BRITISH RAIL

LOCO

C000184867

FORTY-FOURTH EDITION
2002

The Complete Guide to all
Locomotives which operate on
Britain's Mainline Railway and
Eurotunnel Networks

Peter Fox

ISBN 1 902336 21 6

© 2002. Platform 5 Publishing Ltd., 3 Wyvern House, Sark Road, Sheffield,
S2 4HG, England.

CONTENTS

PROVISION OF INFORMATION

This book has been compiled with care to be as accurate as possible, but in some cases official information is not available and the publisher cannot be held responsible for any errors or omissions. We would like to thank the companies and individuals which have been co-operative in supplying information to us. The authors of this series of books will be pleased to receive notification from readers of any inaccuracies readers may find in the series, and also notification of any additional information to supplement our records and thus enhance future editions. Please send comments to:

Peter Fox, Platform 5 Publishing Ltd., Wyvern House, Sark Road, Sheffield, S2 4HG, England.
Tel: 0114 255 2625 Fax: 0114 255 2471
e-mail: peter@platfive.freeserve.co.uk

Both the author and the staff of Platform 5 regret they are unable to answer specific queries regarding locomotives and rolling stock.

This book is updated to 20 November 2001.

UPDATES

An update to all the books in the *British Railways Pocket Book* series is published every month in the new Platform 5 magazine, *entrain*, which contains news and rolling stock information on the railways of Britain and Ireland. For further details of *entrain*, please see the advertisement inside the front cover of this book.

BRITAIN'S RAILWAY SYSTEM

INFRASTRUCTURE & OPERATION

Britain's national railway infrastructure is owned by a public company – Railtrack PLC (now in administration). Many stations and maintenance depots are leased to and operated by Train Operating Companies (TOCs), but some larger stations remain under Railtrack control. The only exception is the infrastructure on the Isle of Wight, which is nationally owned and is leased to the Island Line franchisee.

Trains are operated by TOCs over the Railtrack network, regulated by access agreements between the parties involved. In general, TOCs are responsible for the provision and maintenance of the locomotives, rolling stock and staff necessary for the direct operation of services, whilst Railtrack is responsible for the provision and maintenance of the infrastructure and also for staff needed to regulate the operation of services.

DOMESTIC PASSENGER TRAIN OPERATORS

The large majority of passenger trains are operated by the TOCs on fixed term franchises. Franchise expiry dates are shown in parentheses in the list of franchisees below:

Franchise	Franchisee	Trading Name
Anglia Railways	GB Railways Ltd. (until 4 April 2004)	Anglia Railways
Central Trains	National Express Group PLC (until 1 April 2004)	Central Trains
Chiltern Railways	M40 Trains Ltd. (until 20 July 2003)	Chiltern Railways
Cross Country	Virgin Rail Group Ltd. (until 4 January 2012)	Virgin Trains
Gatwick Express	National Express Group PLC (until 27 April 2011)	Gatwick Express
Great Eastern Railway	First Group PLC (until 4 April 2004)	First Great Eastern
Great Western Trains	First Group PLC (until 3 February 2006)	First Great Western
InterCity East Coast	GNER Holdings Ltd. (until 4 April 2004)	Great North Eastern Railway
InterCity West Coast	Virgin Rail Group Ltd. (until 8 March 2012)	Virgin Trains
Island Line	Stagecoach Holdings PLC (until 12 October 2003)	Island Line
LTS Rail	National Express Group PLC (until 25 May 2011)	c2c
Merseyrail Electrics	Arriva PLC (until 18 February 2003)	Merseyrail Electrics
Midland Main Line	National Express Group PLC (until 27 April 2008)	Midland Mainline

North London Railways	National Express Group PLC (until 1 September 2004)	Silverlink Train Services
North West Regional Railways	First Group PLC (until 1 April 2004)	First North Western
Regional Railways North East	Arriva PLC (until 18 February 2003)	Arriva Trains Northern
Scotrail	National Express Group PLC (until 30 March 2004)	ScotRail
South Central	GOVIA Ltd.§ (until 25 May 2003)	South Central
South Eastern	Connex Transport UK Ltd. (until 12 October 2011)	Connex
South West	Stagecoach Holdings PLC (until 3 February 2023)	South West Trains
Thames	Victory Railways Holdings Ltd. (until 12 April 2004)	Thames Trains
Thameslink	GOVIA Ltd. (until 1 April 2004)	Thameslink Rail
Great Northern	National Express Group PLC (until 31 May 2001)	WAGN
Wales & Borders*	National Express Group PLC (until 30 April 2004)	Wales & Borders Trains
Wessex Trains*	National Express Group PLC (until 30 April 2004)	Cardiff Railways
West Anglia	National Express Group PLC (until 4 April 2004)	WAGN

Notes: * For the present, the existing Wales & West TOC is the legal trading name of Wessex Trains and the Cardiff Railway Company is the legal name for Wales & Borders pending the award of the new Wales & Borders and Wessex franchises.

§ Pending finalisation of new 20-year franchise.

The following operators run non-franchised services only:

Operator	Trading Name	Route
British Airports Authority	Heathrow Express	London Paddington–Heathrow Airport
Hull Trains	Hull Trains	London King's Cross–Hull
West Coast Railway Co.	West Coast Railway	Fort William–Mallaig

INTERNATIONAL PASSENGER OPERATIONS

Eurostar (UK) operates international passenger-only services between the United Kingdom and continental Europe, jointly with French National Railways (SNCF) and Belgian National Railways (SNCB/NMBS). Eurostar (UK) is a subsidiary of London & Continental Railways, which is jointly owned by National Express Group PLC and British Airways.

In addition, a service for the conveyance of accompanied road vehicles through the Channel Tunnel is provided by the tunnel operating company, Eurotunnel.

FREIGHT TRAIN OPERATIONS

The following operators operate freight train services under 'Open Access' arrangements:

English Welsh & Scottish Railway Ltd. (EWS)
Freightliner Ltd.
GB Railfreight Ltd.
Direct Rail Services Ltd.
Mendip Rail Ltd.

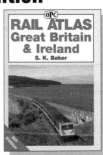

INTRODUCTION

SCOPE

This book contains details of all locomotives which can run on Britain's national railway network, plus those of Eurotunnel. Locomotives which are owned by EWS and Freightliner which have been withdrawn from service and awaiting disposal are now listed in the main list, as are those owned by Fragonset which are awaiting possible restoration to service. Only preserved locomotives which are currently used or are likely to be used on the national network in the foreseeable future are included. Others, which may be Railtrack registered but not at present certified for use, are not included, but will be found in the Platform 5 book, 'Preserved locomotives and Multiple Units'.

LAYOUT OF INFORMATION

Railtrack registered locomotives are listed in numerical order of class number, and then in numerical order of individual locomotives – using current numbers as allocated by the Rolling Stock Library (RSL) – the national registry of rail vehicles. The only exceptions are locomotives numbered in the 89xxx series (see page 9), which are listed under their previous class numbers. Where numbers actually carried are different from those officially allocated, these are noted in class headings where appropriate. Where locomotives have been recently renumbered, the most immediate previous number is shown in parentheses. Each locomotive entry is laid out as in one of the following examples:

RSL No.	Detail	Livery	Owner	Pool	Allocn.	Name
37682	r§	**E**	E	WKAD	TO	Hartlepool Pipe Mill

In some cases where few members of a class are named, names are appended as a separate list at the end of the class listings to save space.

CLASS HEADINGS

Principal details and dimensions are quoted for each class in metric and/or imperial units as considered appropriate bearing in mind common UK usage. Abbreviations used are shown in Section 4.5.

All dimensions and weights are quoted for locomotives in an 'as new' condition with all necessary supplies (e.g. oil, water and sand) on board. Dimensions are quoted in the order length x width. Lengths quoted are over buffers or couplers as appropriate. All widths quoted are maxima. Where two different wheel diameter dimensions are shown, the first refers to powered wheels and the second refers to non-powered wheels.

DETAIL DIFFERENCES

Only detail differences which currently affect the areas and types of train which locomotives may work are shown. All other detail differences are specifically excluded. Where such differences occur within a class or part class, they are shown in the 'Detail' column alongside the individual locomotive number. Standard abbreviations used are:

a	Train air brake equipment only.
b	Drophead buckeye couplers.
c	Scharfenberg couplers.
k	Swinghead automatic combination couplers.
p	Train air, vacuum and electro-pneumatic brakes.
s	Slow Speed Control equipment.
v	Train vacuum brake only.
x	Train air and vacuum brakes ('Dual brakes').
+	Additional fuel tank capacity.
§	Sandite laying equipment.

In all cases use of the above abbreviations indicates the equipment indicated is normally operable. Meaning of non-standard abbreviations and symbols is detailed in individual class headings.

Note: Where a locomotive pool code indicates a detail difference, e.g. as in WBBM which is a special pool for RETB fitted locos, then the fitting is not shown separately.

LIVERY CODES

Livery codes are used to denote the various liveries carried. It is impossible in a publication of this size to list every livery variation which currently exists. In particular items ignored for the purposes of this publication include:

- Minor colour variations.
- Omission of logos.
- All numbering, lettering and branding.

Descriptions quoted are thus a general guide only. Logos as appropriate for each livery are normally deemed to be carried. A complete list of livery codes used appears in Section 4.1.

The various EWS locos and former EWS locos in Railfreight grey codes have now been grouped into one code "F" no matter what logo they may carry.

OWNER CODES

Owner codes are used to denote the owners of locomotives listed. A complete list of owner codes used appears in Section 4.2.

POOL CODES

Locomotives are split into operational groups ('pools') for diagramming and maintenance purposes. The official codes used to denote these pools are shown in this publication. A complete list of the pool codes used appears in Section 4.3.

ALLOCATION & LOCATION CODES

Allocation codes are used in this publication to denote the normal maintenance base of each operational locomotive. However, maintenance may be carried out at other locations and may also be carried out by mobile maintenance teams.

Location codes are used to denote the current actual location of stored vehicles. The designation (S) denotes stored. However, when the loco pool code denotes that a loco is stored then the (S) is not shown.

A complete list of codes and abbreviations appears in Section 4.4.

NAMES

Only names carried with official sanction are listed in this publication. As far as possible names are shown in UPPER/lower case characters as actually shown on the name carried on the locomotive. Names known to be carried on one are shown by a superscript [1] (e.g. Back Tor[1]).

GENERAL INFORMATION

CLASSIFICATION AND NUMBERING

All locomotives are classified and allocated numbers by the Rolling Stock Library under the TOPS numbering system, introduced in 1972. This comprises a two-digit class number followed by a three-digit serial number. Where the actual number carried by a locomotive differs from the allocated number, or where an additional number is carried to the allocated number, this is shown by a note in the class heading.

For diesel locomotives, class numbers offer an indication of engine horsepower as shown in the table below.

Class No. Range	Engine h.p.
01–14	0–799
15–20	800–1000
21–31	1001–1499
32–39	1500–1999
40–54, 57	2000–2999
55–56, 58–69	3000+

For electric locomotives class numbers are allocated in ascending numerical order under the following scheme:

Class 70–80	direct current and d.c./diesel dual system locomotives.
Class 81 onwards	alternating current and a.c./d.c. dual system locos.

Numbers in the 89xxx series (except 89001) are allocated by the Rolling Stock Library to locomotives which have been de-registered but subsequently re-registered for use on the Railtrack network and whose original number has already been re-used. 89xxx numbers are normally only carried inside locomotive cabs and are not carried externally in normal circumstances.

WHEEL ARRANGEMENT

For main line locomotives the number of driven axles on a bogie or frame is denoted by a letter (A = 1, B = 2, C = 3 etc.) and the number of non-powered axles is denoted by a number. The use of the letter 'o' after a letter indicates each axle is individually powered, whilst the '+' symbol indicates bogies are inter-coupled.

For shunting locomotives, the Whyte notation is used. In this notation the number of leading wheels are given, followed by the number of driving wheels and then the trailing wheels.

HAULAGE CAPABILITY OF DIESEL LOCOMOTIVES

The haulage capability of a diesel locomotive depends upon three basic factors:

1. Adhesive weight. The greater the weight on the driving wheels, the greater the adhesion and more tractive power can be applied before wheelslip occurs.

2. The characteristics of its transmission. To start a train the locomotive has to exert a pull at standstill. A direct drive diesel engine cannot do this, hence the need for transmission. This may be mechanical, hydraulic or electric. The present British Standard for locomotives is electric transmission. Here the diesel engine drives a generator or alternator and the current produced is fed to the traction motors. The force produced by each driven wheel depends on the current in its traction motor. In other words, the larger the current, the harder it pulls. As the locomotive speed increases, the current in the traction motor falls, hence the *Maximum Tractive Effort* is the maximum force at its wheels the locomotive can exert at a standstill. The electrical equipment cannot take such high currents for long without overheating. Hence the *Continuous Tractive Effort* is quoted which represents the current which the equipment can take continuously.

3. The power of its engine. Not all power reaches the rail, as electrical machines are approximately 90% efficient. As the electrical energy passes through two such machines (the generator or alternator and the traction motors), the *Power at Rail* is approximately 81% (90% of 90%) of the engine power, less a further amount used for auxiliary equipment such as radiator fans, traction motor blowers, air compressors, battery charging, cab heating, Electric Train Supply (ETS) etc. The power of the locomotive is proportional to the tractive effort times the speed. Hence when on full power there is a speed corresponding to the continuous tractive effort.

HAULAGE CAPABILITY OF ELECTRIC LOCOMOTIVES

Unlike a diesel locomotive, an electric locomotive does not develop its power on board and its performance is determined only by two factors, namely its weight and the characteristics of its electrical equipment. Whereas a diesel locomotive tends to be a constant power machine, the power of an electric locomotive varies considerably. Up to a certain speed it can produce virtually a constant tractive effort. Hence power rises with speed according to the formula given in section three above, until a maximum speed is reached at which tractive effort falls, such that the power also falls. Hence the power at the speed corresponding to the maximum tractive effort is lower than the maximum speed.

BRAKE FORCE

The brake force is a measure of the braking power of a locomotive. This is shown on the locomotive data panels so operating staff can ensure sufficient brake power is available on freight trains.

ELECTRIC TRAIN SUPPLY (ETS)

A number of locomotives are equipped to provide a supply of electricity to the train being hauled to power auxiliaries such as heating, cooling fans, air conditioning and kitchen equipment. ETS is provided from the locomotive by means of a separate alternator (except Class 33 locos, which have a d.c. generator). The ETS index of a locomotive is a measure of the electrical power available for train supply.

Similarly, most loco-hauled coaches also have an ETS index, which in this case is a measure of the power required to operate equipment mounted in the coach. The sum of the ETS indices of all the hauled vehicles in a train must not exceed the ETS index of the locomotive.

ETS is commonly (but incorrectly) known as ETH (Electric Train Heating), which is a throwback to the days before loco-hauled coaches were equipped with electrically powered auxiliary equipment other than for train heating.

ROUTE AVAILABILITY (RA)

This is a measure of a railway vehicle's axle load. The higher the axle load of a vehicle, the higher the RA number on a scale from 1 to 10. Each Railtrack route has a RA number and in general no vehicle with a higher RA number may travel on that route without special clearance. A map showing route availability on all routes is published on the Railtrack internet web site.

MULTIPLE & PUSH-PULL WORKING

Multiple working between vehicles (i.e. two or more powered vehicles being driven from one cab) is facilitated by jumper cables connecting the vehicles. However, not all types are compatible with each other, and a number of different systems are in use, each system being incompatible with any other.

Association of American Railroads (AAR) System: Classes 59, 66, and 67.
Blue Star Coupling Code: Classes 20, 25, 31, 33, & 37.
Green Circle Coupling Code: Class 47 (not all equipped).
Orange Square Coupling Code: Class 50.
Red Diamond Coupling Code: Classes 56 and 58.
SR System: Classes 33/1, 73 and various electric multiple units.
Within Own Class only: Classes 43 and 60.

Many locomotives use a time-division multiplex (TDM) system for push-pull and multiple working which utilises the existing RCH jumper cables fitted to coaching stock vehicles. Previously these cables had only been used to control train lighting and public address systems.

Class 47 locos 47701–47717 were equipped with a older non-standard TDM system.

1. DIESEL LOCOMOTIVES

Note: The 01/5 series has been allocated for shunting locomotives of various types which may operate on the Railtrack network. Only those actually registered on TOPS, or ex-BR locos are included here.

SERIES 01/5   H-B/CATERPILLAR   0-6-0

Built: 1971 by The Hunslet Engine Company at Leeds (Works No. 7018), for the National Coal Board, Western Area (No. 8D). Subsequently sold to Hunslet-Barclay, Kilmarnock and rebuilt prior to sale to The Felixstowe Dock and Railway Company in 1999. Registered for use on the Railtrack network in 1999. Normally used at Felixstowe South Container Terminal.
Engine: Caterpillar 3412C DITA of 475 kW (640 h.p.) at ? r.p.m.
Transmission: Hydraulic. Twin Disc 13800 series torque converter coupled to a Hunslet final drive.
Maximum Tractive Effort: 180 kN (40365 lbf).
Train Brakes: Air.
Brake Force: 48 t.
Weight: 64.3 t.
Design Speed: 15 m.p.h.
Fuel Capacity: 930 litres.
Train Supply: Not equipped.
Dimensions: 3.95 x 2.51 m.
Wheel Diameter: 1143 mm.
Maximum Speed: 15 m.p.h.
RA: 7.
Multiple Working: Not equipped.
Non standard numbering: Also carries number H4323.

| 01531 | **FX** | FX | MBDL | FX | COLONEL TOMLINE |

SERIES 01/5   ENGLISH ELECTRIC/RR   0-4-0

Built: 1966 by English Electric at Vulcan Foundry, Newton le Willows (Works No. D1122), for the Central Electricity Generating Board at Croydon 'B' Power Station (No. 2). Subsequently acquired by RFS(E), Doncaster (now Wabtec). Registered for use on the Railtrack network in 2000, and hired to Aggregate Industries UK for use at Croft Quarry, Leicestershire.
Engine: ? of 235 kW (315 h.p.) at ? r.p.m.
Transmission: Hydraulic.
Maximum Tractive Effort:
Train Brakes: Air.
Brake Force: 10 t.
Weight: 24.0 t.
Design Speed: 10 m.p.h.
Fuel Capacity: 1365 litres.
Train Supply: Not equipped.
Dimensions: 7.32 x ? m.
Wheel Diameter:
Maximum Speed: 10 m.p.h.
RA: 0.
Multiple Working: Not equipped.
Non standard livery: RFS(E) livery of blue, lined out in silver.

| 01551 | **0** | WA | MBDL | ZB |

SERIES 01/5   HNRC/ROLLS-ROYCE   0-6-0

Built: 1966 by Thomas Hill at Vanguard Works, Kilnhurst (Works No. 167V), for ICI Billingham (No. D3). Subsequently sold to Harry Needle Railroad

Company in 1995 and rebuilt 2000. Registered for use on the Railtrack network in 2000, and hired to Creative Logistics, for use at Salford International Railfreight Terminal.
Engine: Rolls Royce 8-cylinder of 275 kW (370 h.p.) at ? r.p.m.
Transmission: Hydraulic. Twin Disc 11800 torque converter coupled to a RF final drive unit.
Maximum Tractive Effort:
Train Brakes: Air.

Brake Force: 19 t.	**Dimensions:** 9.14 x ? m.
Weight: 49.0 t.	**Wheel Diameter:**
Design Speed: 10 m.p.h.	**Maximum Speed:** 10 m.p.h.
Fuel Capacity: 1360 litres.	**RA:** 5.
Train Supply: Not equipped.	**Multiple Working:** Not equipped.

Non standard livery: Creative Logistics livery of blue and green.

01552   **0**   HN   HNRL   BH

SERIES 01/5   BR/ENGLISH ELECTRIC   0-6-0

Built: 1950 by BR at Derby Locomotive Works to LMS design as BR 12082. Withdrawn from service in 1971 and sold to Shellstar (UK), Ince (later UK Fertilisers) in 1972. Purchased by Harry Needle in 19??, and registered for use on the Railtrack network in 2000. Part of the Harry Needle Railroad Company hire fleet. **Engine:** English Electric 6KT of 260 kW (350 h.p.) at 600 r.p.m.
Main Generator: English Electric 801.
Traction Motors: Two English Electric 506.
Maximum Tractive Effort: 156 kN (35000 lbf).
Continuous Tractive Effort: ? at 8.5 m.p.h.

Power at Rail:	**Train Brakes:** Air.
Brake Force: 19 t.	**Dimensions:** 8.88 x 2.59 m.
Weight: 48.60 t.	**Wheel Diameter:** 1232 mm.
Design Speed: 20 m.p.h.	**Maximum Speed:** 20 m.p.h.
Fuel Capacity: 3000 litres.	**RA:** 5.
Train Supply: Not equipped.	**Multiple Working:** Not equipped.

Non-standard numbering: Also carries original number 12082.

01553 (12082)   **HN**   HN HNRL   BH

CLASS 03   BR/GARDNER   0-6-0

Built: 1962 by BR at Swindon Works. Normally used at Hornsey T&RSMD.
Engine: Gardner 8L3 of 152 kW (204 h.p.) at 1200 r.p.m.
Transmission: Mechanical. Fluidrive type 23 hydraulic coupling to Wilson-Drewry CA5R7 gearbox with SCG type RF11 final drive.
Maximum Tractive Effort: 68 kN (15300 lbf).
Continuous Tractive Effort: 68 kN (15300 lbf) at 3.75 m.p.h.
Train Brakes: Air & vacuum.

Brake Force: 13 t.	**Dimensions:** 7.93 x 2.59 m.
Weight: 31.3 t.	**Wheel Diameter:** 1092 mm.
Design Speed: 28.5 m.p.h.	**Maximum Speed:** 28.5 m.p.h.
Fuel Capacity: 1364 litres.	**RA:** 1.
Train Supply: Not equipped.	**Multiple Working:** Not equipped.

Originally numbered D 2179.

03179   **WN** WN HQXX   HE

CLASS 07 RUSTON & HORNSBY/PAXMAN 0-6-0

Built: 1962 by Ruston & Hornsby, Lincoln, as BR D2985 for shunting duties in Southampton Docks. Withdrawn from service in 1977 and sold to Tilsley & Lovatt, Stoke-on-Trent in 1978. Resold to Staveley Lime Company (later Peakstone Ltd.), Peak Dale, in 1978. Purchased by Harry Needle in 1989 and registered for use on the Railtrack network in 2000. Part of the Harry Needle Railroad Company hire fleet.
Engine: Paxman 6RPHL Mk. 3 of 204 kW (275 h.p.) at 1360 r.p.m.
Main Generator: AEI RTB 6652.
Traction Motors: AEI RTA 6652.
Maximum Tractive Effort: 126 kN (28240 lbf).
Continuous Tractive Effort: ? at 4.4 m.p.h.

Power at Rail:	**Train Brakes:** Air.
Brake Force: 21 t.	**Dimensions:** 8.13 x 2.57 m.
Weight: 42.25 t.	**Wheel Diameter:** 1067 mm.
Design Speed: 20 m.p.h.	**Maximum Speed:** 20 m.p.h.
Fuel Capacity:	**RA:** 6.
Train Supply: Not equipped.	**Multiple Working:** Not equipped.

Originally numbered D 2985.

07001   **HN** HN HNRL   BH

CLASS 08   BR/ENGLISH ELECTRIC   0-6-0

Built: 1955–62 by BR at Crewe, Darlington, Derby Locomotive, Doncaster or Horwich Works.
Engine: English Electric 6KT of 298 kW (400 h.p.) at 680 r.p.m.
Main Generator: English Electric 801.
Traction Motors: Two English Electric 506.
Maximum Tractive Effort: 156 kN (35000 lbf).
Continuous Tractive Effort: 49 kN (11100 lbf) at 8.8 m.p.h.

Power At Rail: 194 kW (260 h.p.).	**Train Brakes:** Air & vacuum.
Brake Force: 19 t.	**Dimensions:** 8.92 x 2.59 m.
Weight: 49.6–50.4 t.	**Wheel Diameter:** 1372 mm.
Design Speed: 20 m.p.h.	**Maximum Speed:** 15 m.p.h.
Fuel Capacity: 3037 litres.	**RA:** 5.
Train Supply: Not equipped.	**Multiple Working:** Not equipped.

Notes: † – Equipped with remote control (Hima Sella system) for working at Allied Steel & Wire, Cardiff.
§ – Equipped with remote control (Cattron system) for evaluation purposes.

Non-standard liveries/numbering:

08414 is as **DG**, but with BR & Railfreight Distribution logos and large bodyside numbers. Also carries number D3529.
08460 is light grey with black underframe, cab doors, window surrounds and roof. Also carries number D3575.
08500 is red, lined out in black & white. Also carries bodyside number 1.

08527 is light grey with a black roof, blue bodyside stripe and "Ilford Level 5" branding.
08573 is light grey and unnumbered.
08593 is Great Eastern Railway style blue. Also carries number D3760.
08601 is London Midland & Scottish Railway style black.
08616 carries number 3783.
08617 is in Virgin Trains "Pitstop" livery of black with a large red and black bodyside flag.
08642 is London & South Western Railway style black. Also carries number D3809.
08649 is grey with blue, white and red stripes and WTL logo. Also carries number D3816.
08682 is dark blue with a grey roof.
08715 is "Dayglo" orange.
08721 is as **B**, but with a red and yellow stripe.
08785 is silver grey.
08801 carries number 801.
08805 is London Midland & Scottish Railway style maroon. Also carries number 3973.
08809 is light grey with orange lettering.
08834 is in RFS(E) livery of blue with silver lining.
08879 is green and black with Railfreight Distribution logos.
08883 is Caledonian Railway style blue.
08928 is as **F0** with large bodyside numbers and light blue solebar.

Originally numbered in series D 3000–4192.

Class 08/0. Standard Design.

08077		**0**	P	DFLS	FD	08482 a	**F**	E	WSAS	OC
08308 a	**SS**	RT	MOLO	IS	08483 a	**GL**	FG	HJXX	PM
08331		**GN**	WA	RFSH	EC	08484 a	**DG**	RC	KWSW	ZN
08375 a	**RT**	RT	DFLS	FD	08485 a	**B**	EF	WSNW	AN
08389 a	**B**	EF	WSNE	IM	08489 a	**F**	E	WSWX	WA
08393 a	**FE**	EF	WSAS	OC	08492 a	**B**	E	WSYX	ML
08397 a	**E**	E	WSNW	AN	08493 a	**B**	E	WSYX	CF
08401 a	**DG**	E	WSNE	IM	08495		**E**	E	WSNE	IM
08402 a	**E**	E	WSSC	ML	08499 a	**E**	E	WSGW	CF
08405 a	**DG**	E	WSNE	IM	08500		**0**	E	WSGW	CF
08410 a	**GL**	FG	HJSL	LA	08506 a	**B**	E	WSAS	OC
08411 a	**B**	E	WSSC	ML	08507 a	**HN**	HN	HNRL	CZ
08414 a	**0**	E	WSWX	OC	08509 a	**F**	E	WSWX	IM
08417 a	**B**	SO	CDJD	MD	08510 a	**B**	E	WSNE	IM
08418 a	**F**	E	WSMD	TO	08511 a	**E**	E	WSMD	TO
08428 a	**E**	E	WSNE	IM	08512 a	**F**	E	WSNE	IM
08441 a	**E**	E	WSSC	ML	08514 a	**E**	E	WSNE	IM
08442 a	**F**	E	WSNE	IM	08516 a	**DG**	E	WSMD	TO
08451		**B**	VW	HFSN	WN	08523		**ML**	E	WSXX	CD
08454		**VP**	VW	HFSN	WN	08525		**F**	MA	HISL	NL
08460 a	**0**	E	WSNW	AN	08526		**E**	E	WSAS	OC
08466 at	**E**	E	WSAW	CF	08527		**0**	BT	KCSI	ZI
08472 a	**BR**	WA	RFSH	EC	08528		**DG**	E	WSMD	TO
08480 a	**G**	E	WSGW	CF	08529		**B**	E	WSXX	DR
08481		**B**	E	WSAW	CF	08530		**DG**	P	DFLS	FD

No.						
08531	a	**DG**	P	DFLS	FD	
08534		**DG**	E	WSSC	ML	
08535		**DG**	EF	WSXX	CD	
08536		**B**	MA	HISE	DY	(S)
08538		**DG**	E	WSMD	TO	
08540		**DG**	E	WSMD	TO	
08541		**DG**	E	WSXX	OC	
08542		**F**	E	WSXX	BS	
08543		**DG**	E	WSMD	TO	
08561		**B**	E	WSNW	AN	
08567		**B**	E	WSMD	TO	
08568	a	**B**	RC	KGSS	ZH	(S)
08569		**E**	EF	WSMD	TO	
08571	a	**B**	WA	RFSH	WH	
08573		**0**	RT	KCSI	ZI	
08575		**FL**	P	DFLS	FD	
08576		**B**	E	WSXX	CF	
08577		**B**	E	WSNE	IM	
08578		**RG**	E	WSWX	FB	
08580		**B**	E	WSMD	TO	
08582	a	**DG**	E	WSNE	IM	
08585		**FL**	P	DFLS	FD	
08587		**B**	E	WSNE	IM	
08588		**BR**	MA	HISL	NL	(S)
08593		**0**	E	WSSC	ML	
08596	a†	**WA**	WA	RFSH	ZB	
08597		**B**	E	WSNE	IM	
08599		**B**	E	WSNE	IM	
08601		**0**	E	WSXX	AN	
08605		**B**	E	WSNE	IM	
08611		**V**	VW	HFSL	LO	
08613		**K**	RT		ZI	
08616		**GW**	MA	HGSS	TS	
08617		**0**	VW	HFSN	WN	
08623		**B**	E	WSMD	TO	
08624		**B**	P	DFLS	FD	
08628		**B**	E	WSXX	SY	
08629		**RP**	RC	KWSW	ZN	
08630		**E**	E	WSSC	ML	
08631		**N**	PO	SDFR	NC	
08632		**E**	E	WSNW	AN	
08633		**RX**	E	WSNE	IM	
08635		**B**	E	WSAS	OC	
08641		**DG**	FG	HJSL	LA	
08642		**0**	P	DFLS	SZ	
08643		**GL**	FG	HJXX	PM	
08644		**IM**	FG	HJSL	LA	
08645		**WA**	FG	HJSL	LA	
08646		**F**	E	WSAS	OC	
08648		**DG**	FG	HJSL	LA	(S)
08649		**0**	AM	KESE	ZG	
08651	a	**DG**	E	WSAW	CF	
08653		**FE**	EF	WSGW	CF	
08655		**F**	EF	WSNE	IM	
08661	a	**F**	EF	WSYX	AN	
08662		**B**	E	WSNE	IM	
08663	a	**GL**	FG	HJSL	LA	
08664		**E**	E	WSAS	OC	
08665		**B**	E	WSNW	AN	
08666		**B**	E	WSNW	AN	
08669	a		WA	HJSL	LA	
08670	a	**E**	E	WSSC	ML	
08673		**IM**	E	WSYX	AN	
08675		**F**	E	WSXX	ML	
08676		**B**	E	WSNE	IM	
08678		**0**	WC	SDFR	DY	
08682		**0**	BT	KDSD	ZF	
08683		**B**	E	WSMD	TO	
08685		**B**	E	WSGW	CF	
08689	a	**E**	E	WSNE	IM	
08690		**MA**	MA	HISE	DY	
08691		**G**	WA	DFLS	FD	
08694	a	**E**	EF	WSAS	OC	
08695	a	**E**	E	WSMD	TO	
08696	a	**V**	VW	HFSL	LO	
08697		**B**	MA	HISE	DY	(S)
08698	a	**E**	E	WSMD	TO	
08701	a	**RX**	E	WSNW	AN	
08702		**B**	E	WSXX	ZB	
08703	a	**B**	EF	WSWX	FB	
08706		**B**	E	WSMD	TO	
08709		**B**	E	WSNW	AN	
08711		**RX**	E	WSAS	OC	
08714		**E**	E	WSMD	TO	
08715	v	**0**	E	WSWX	FB	
08720	a	**E**	E	WSSC	ML	
08721		**0**	VW	HFSL	LO	
08724		**WA**	WA	HBSH	NL	
08730		**K**	RC	KGSS	ZH	
08735		**DG**	E	WSWX	DR	
08737	a	**FE**	EF	WSNW	AN	
08738		**E**	E	WSNW	AN	
08739		**B**	EF	WSXX	AN	
08740		**F**	E	WSWX	FB	
08742		**RX**	E	WSMD	TO	
08743		**EN**	EN	MBDL	BG	
08745		**FE**	P	DFLS	CD	(S)
08746		**DG**	E	WSXX	DR	
08750	a	**0**	RT	MOLO	ZB	
08751		**F**	EF	WSYX	ZB	
08752	†	**CE**	E	WSAW	CF	
08754		**FL**	RT	MOLO	AN	

▲ Class 08 shunter 08818 in blue livery travels light from the sidings to the stabling point at Ipswich on 09/09/1999. **Chris Booth**

▼ Class 09 shunter 09016 in departmental grey livery at Plymouth station on 30/05/2001. **Allan Brooks**

DRS Class 20s 20906 and 20904 in blue livery with red solebar stripes are seen at Winwick Quay on the West Coast Main Line with the 15.12 Valley–Sellafield nuclear flasks on 08/08/2000. **Doug Birmingham**

▲ Fragonset Class 31/4s 31468 'HYDRA' and 31459 'CERBERUS' top-and-tail the 13.35 Norwich–Yarmouth at Acle on 19/08/2000.   **Dr Iain C. Scotchman**

▼ The 'Marshes Marauder' railtour on 07/04/2001 is seen approaching Medley Crossing returning from Dungeness hauled by red-liveried Class 33/0 No. 33021 'Eastleigh'.   **Ian G. Feather**

▲ Class 37s Nos. 37886 'Sir Dyfed/County of Dyfed' and 37707 at Newport with a 'Pathfinder' railtour on 03/06/2001. **Andy Flowers**

▼ First Great Western HST (power cars 43124 + 43040) passes Dawlish with the 06.40 Penzance–London Paddington on 28/07/2001. **Hugh Ballantyne**

▲ Fragonset Class 45/1 No. 45112 leaves Bristol Temple Meads with a Lancaster–Penzance excursion on 21/07/2001. **John Chalcraft**

▼ One of Freightliner's dwindling number of 47s in service, 47358, approaches Doncaster with 4L85 from Leeds to Ipswich on 07/06/2000. This loco has just been taken out of service. **Chris Booth**

Virgin-liveried Class 47 No. 47844 at the head of the 09.20 Brighton–Edinburgh on 22/07/2000 at Horwich Fork Jn., Blackrod.
Tom Heavyside

▲ EWS-liveried Class 56 No. 56060 passes signals at Maltby Colliery South on 30/12/2000 on the South Yorkshire Joint line, which runs between Doncaster and Shireoaks, with a Harworth–Cottam m.g.r. train. **Chris Booth**

▼ Class 57 No. 57004 'Freightliner Quality' works the 13.04 Crewe Basford Hall–Southampton past Norton Bridge on 22/07/2000. **Hugh Ballantyne**

The unique Class 57/6 57601 in a special Porterbrook livery approaches Parsons Tunnel, Teignmouth with the 09.20 Plymouth–London Paddington on 28/08/2001.
Russell Ayre

08756		DG	E	WSXX	CF		08867		K	E	WSWX	DE

No.		C1	C2	C3	C4		No.		C1	C2	C3	C4
08756		**DG**	E	WSXX	CF		08867		**K**	E	WSWX	DE
08757		**E**	E	WSMD	TO		08868		**B**	HN	DFLS	FD
08758		**B**	E	WSXX	FB		08869		**G**	CR	CROL	NC
08762		**B**	RT	MOLO	FX		08870		**RL**	RL	MBDL	ZP
08765		**DG**	E	WSMD	TO		08871		**CR**	CR	CREL	NC
08768		**B**	E	WSYX	ML		08872		**DG**	EF	WSAS	OC
08770	a	**DG**	E	WSAW	CF		08873		**RX**	RT	MOLO	CP
08775		**E**	E	WSAS	OC		08874		**SL**	RT	MOLO	BY
08776	a	**DG**	E	WSAS	OC		08877		**DG**	E	WSWX	SP
08780		**K**	FG	HJSE	LE		08879		**0**	EF	WSNE	IM
08782	a	**E**	E	WSNW	AN		08880		**B**	E	WSXX	AN
08783		**B**	E	WSAS	OC		08881		**DG**	E	WSSC	ML
08784		**B**	EF	WSNW	AN		08882		**B**	E	WSYX	FB
08785	a	**0**	P	DFLS	FD		08883		**0**	E	WSSC	ML
08786	a	**DG**	E	WSAS	OC		08884		**B**	E	WSMD	TO
08788		**RT**	RT	MOLO	IS		08886	§	**E**	E	WSNE	IM
08790		**B**	VW	HFSL	LO		08887	a	**VP**	VW	HFSL	LO
08792		**F**	E	WSGW	CF		08888		**E**	E	WSMD	TO
08795		**FG**	FG	HJSE	LE		08890		**DG**	E	WSAS	OC
08798		**B**	E	WSGW	CF		08891		**B**	P	DFLS	FD
08799	a	**E**	EF	WSAS	OC		08892		**GN**	WA	RFSH	BN
08801		**B**	E	WSXX	CF		08893		**DG**	E	WSYX	ZB
08802		**RX**	E	WSNW	AN		08894		**B**	E	WSXX	AN
08804		**E**	E	WSAS	OC		08896		**E**	E	WSAW	CF
08805		**0**	MA	HGSS	TS		08897		**E**	E	WSNW	AN
08806	a	**F**	E	WSXX	IM		08899		**MM**	MA	HISE	DY
08807		**BR**	E	WSSC	ML		08900		**DG**	E	WSAS	OC
08809		**0**	HN	DFLS	FD		08901		**B**	E	WSYX	FB
08810	a	**AR**	CR	CREL	NC		08902		**B**	EF	WSXX	AN
08813	a	**DG**	E	WSYX	TE		08903		**EN**	EN	MBDL	BG
08815		**B**	E	WSYX	AN		08904		**B**	E	WSGW	CF
08817		**BR**	E	WSXX	AN		08905		**E**	EF	WSMD	TO
08818		**B**	HN	HNRL	BH		08906		**B**	E	WSXX	ML
08819		**DG**	E	WSXX	CF		08907		**LW**	EF	WSWX	CF
08822		**GL**	FG	HJXX	OO		08908		**MM**	MA	HISL	NL
08824	ak	**F**	E	WSNE	IM		08909		**ML**	E	WSNW	AN
08825	a	**B**	EF	WSXX	OC		08910		**B**	E	WSSC	ML
08827	a	**B**	E	WSYX	ML		08911		**DG**	E	WSNE	IM
08828	a	**E**	E	WSGW	CF		08912		**B**	E	WSNW	AN
08830		**LW**	CA	HLSV	CP		08913		**DG**	EF	WSGW	CF
08834		**0**	WA	HBSH	BN		08914		**B**	E	WSXX	ZB
08836		**GL**	FG	HJXX	OO		08915		**F**	E	WSNW	AN
08837		**DG**	EF	WSXX	AN		08918		**DG**	E	WSAS	OC
08842		**E**	EF	WSNW	AN		08919		**RX**	E	WSAS	OC
08844		**B**	EF	WSNE	IM		08920		**F**	E	WSMD	TO
08847		**B**	CR	CROL	LB		08921	†	**E**	E	WSAS	CF
08853	a	**B**	WA	RFSH	ZB		08922		**DG**	E	WSNW	AN
08854	†	**E**	E	WSAW	CF		08924		**DG**	E	WSXX	ZB
08856		**B**	EF	WSGW	CF		08925		**B**	E	WSWX	AN
08865		**B**	E	WSAS	OC		08926		**DG**	EF	WSXX	AN
08866		**B**	E	WSNW	AN		08927		**B**	E	WSSC	ML

08928	**0**	CR	CROL	LB		08946	**FE**	EF	WSNW	AN
08931	**B**	E	WSYX	FB		08947	**B**	E	WSAS	OC
08932	**B**	E	WSXX	CD		08948 c	**EP**	EU	GPSS	OC
08933	**E**	VP	WSSC	ML		08950	**IM**	MA	HISL	NL (S)
08934 a	**VP**	VW	HFSN	WN		08951 †	**DG**	EF	WSAW	CF
08936		HN	HNRL	DY		08953 a	**DG**	E	WSNE	IM
08939	**B**	EF	WSMD	TO		08954	**F**	E	WSNE	IM
08940	**B**	E	WSYX	AN		08955	**F**	E	WSXX	CF
08941	**B**	E	WSGW	CF		08956	**B**	SO	CDJD	DY
08942	**B**	E	WSXX	ZB		08957	**E**	E	WSYX	CF

Names:

08629 BRML WOLVERTON LEVEL 5	08804 Richard J. Wenham
08649 G.H. Stratton	08869 THE CANARY
08682 Lionheart	08879 Sheffield Childrens Hospital
08694 PAT BARR	08896 STEPHEN DENT
08701 The Sorter	08903 John W Antill
08714 Cambridge	08905 Danny Daniels
08743 Bryan Turner	08919 Steep Holm
08790 M.A. SMITH	08950 Neville Hill 1st

Class 08/9. Reduced height cab. Converted 1985–87 by BR at Landore T&RSMD.

08993	**E**	E	WSGW	CF	ASHBURNHAM
08994 a	**E**	E	WSGW	CF	GWENDRAETH
08995 a	**E**	E	WSGW	CF	KIDWELLY

CLASS 09   BR/ENGLISH ELECTRIC   0-6-0

Built: 1959–62 by BR at Darlington or Horwich Works.
Engine: English Electric 6KT of 298 kW (400 h.p.) at 680 r.p.m.
Main Generator: English Electric 801.
Traction Motors: English Electric 506.
Maximum Tractive Effort: 111 kN (25000 lbf).
Continuous Tractive Effort: 39 kN (8800 lbf) at 11.6 m.p.h.
Power At Rail: 201 kW (269 h.p.).   **Train Brakes:** Air & vacuum.
Brake Force: 19 t.   **Dimensions:** 8.92 x 2.59 m.
Weight: 50 t.   **Wheel Diameter:** 1372 mm.
Design Speed: 27 m.p.h.   **Maximum Speed:** 27 m.p.h.
Fuel Capacity: 3037 litres.   **RA:** 5.
Train Supply: Not equipped.   **Multiple Working:** Not equipped.

Class 09/0 were originally numbered D 3665–71, 3719–21, 4099–4114.

Class 09/0. Built as Class 09.

09001	**E**	E	WSGW	CF	
09003	**E**	E	WSGW	CF	
09005	**E**	E	WSNE	IM	
09006	**ML**	E	WSAS	OC	
09007	**ML**	E	WSNE	IM	
09008	**E**	E	WSGW	CF	
09009	**E**	E	WSAS	OC	Three Bridges C.E.D.

09010	**DG**	E	WSAS	OC	
09011	**DG**	EF	WSGW	CF	
09012	**DG**	E	WSAS	OC	Dick Hardy
09013	**DG**	E	WSGW	CF	
09014	**DG**	E	WSNE	IM	
09015	**DG**	E	WSGW	CF	
09016	**DG**	E	WSGW	CF	
09017	**E**	E	WSGW	CF	
09018	**E**	E	WSAS	OC	
09019	**ML**	E	WSAS	OC	
09020	**B**	E	WSXX	ZB	
09021	**E**	EF	WSMD	TO	
09022 a	**E**	EF	WSNW	AN	
09023 a	**E**	E	WSNE	IM	
09024	**ML**	E	WSAS	OC	
09025	**CX**	SC	HWSU	BI	
09026	**G**	SC	HWSU	BI	William Pearson

Class 09/1. Converted from Class 08/0. 110 V electrical equipment.

Converted: 1992–93 by RFS Industries, Kilnhurst.

09101	(08833)		**DG**	E	WSGW	CF
09102	(08832)		**DG**	E	WSGW	CF
09103	(08766)		**DG**	E	WSMD	TO
09104	(08749)		**DG**	E	WSSC	ML
09105	(08835)		**DG**	E	WSGW	CF
09106	(08759)		**DG**	E	WSNE	IM
09107	(08845)		**DG**	E	WSNE	IM

Class 09/2. Converted from Class 08. 90 V electrical equipment.

Converted: 1992 by RFS Industries, Kilnhurst.

09201	(08421)	ak	**DG**	E	WSNE	IM
09202	(08732)		**DG**	E	WSNE	IM
09203	(08781)		**DG**	E	WSGW	CF
09204	(08717)		**DG**	E	WSNE	IM
09205	(08620)		**DG**	E	WSSC	ML

CLASS 20   ENGLISH ELECTRIC   Bo-Bo

Built: 1957–68 by English Electric Company at Vulcan Foundry, Newton le Willows or by Robert Stephenson & Hawthorn at Darlington.
Engine: English Electric 8SVT Mk. II of 746 kW (1000 h.p.) at 850 r.p.m.
Main Generator: English Electric 819/3C.
Traction Motors: English Electric 526/5D or 526/8D.
Maximum Tractive Effort: 187 kN (42000 lbf).
Continuous Tractive Effort: 111 kN (25000 lbf) at 11 m.p.h.

Power At Rail: 574 kW (770 h.p.).	**Train Brakes:** Air & vacuum.
Brake Force: 35 t.	**Dimensions:** 14.25 x 2.67 m.
Weight: 73.4–73.5 t.	**Wheel Diameter:** 1092 mm.
Design Speed: 75 m.p.h.	**Maximum Speed:** 60 m.p.h.
Fuel Capacity: 1727 litres.	**RA:** 5.

Train Supply: Not equipped.   **Multiple Working:** Blue Star.

Non-standard liveries:

20092 is in Central Services grey & red livery.
20905 is in Hunslet-Barclay two-tone grey with red solebar.

Originally numbered in series D 8007–8190, 8315–8325.

Class 20/0. Standard Design.

20007	**B**	DR	XHSS	ZB
20016	**B**	DR		LT (S)
20032	**B**	DR	XHSS	ZB
20057	**B**	DR		LT (S)
20066	**B**	DR		LT (S)
20073	**B**	DR		LT (S)
20081	**B**	DR		LT (S)
20088	**F**	DR	XHSS	SD
20092	**0**	DR		LT (S)
20094	**F**	DR	XHSS	KM
20105	**F**	DR		ZB (S)
20108	**F**	DR	XHSS	SD
20113	**F**	DR	XHSS	KM
20121	**B**	DR	XHSS	ZB
20132	**B**	DR		LT (S)
20133	**F**	DR		ZB (S)
20135	**B**	DR		KM
20138	**F**	DR		LT (S)
20145	**F**	DR		ZB (S)
20159	**F**	DR		ZB (S)
20165	**FR**	DR	XHSS	KM
20175	**F**	DR	XHSS	KM
20209	**F**	DR	XHSS	KM
20215	**B**	DR	XHSS	ZB

Class 20/3. Direct Rail Services refurbished locos. Details as Class 20/0 except:

Refurbished: 1995–96 by Brush Traction at Loughborough (20301–305) or 1997–98 by RFS(E) at Doncaster (20306–315). Disc indicators or headcode panels removed.
Train Brakes: Air.   **Maximum Speed:** 75 m.p.h.
Brake Force: 31 t.   **Fuel Capacity:** 2900 (+ 4909) litres.
Multiple Working: Blue Star (20301–305 at nose end only).

20301	(20047)	+	**DR**	DR	XHSD	KM	Max Joule 1958–1999
20302	(20084)		**DR**	DR	XHSD	KM	
20303	(20127)	+	**DR**	DR	XHSD	KM	
20304	(20120)		**DR**	DR	XHSD	KM	
20305	(20095)		**DR**	DR	XHSD	KM	
20306	(20131)	+	**DR**	DR	XHSD	KM	
20307	(20128)	+	**DR**	DR	XHSD	KM	
20308	(20187)	+	**DR**	DR	XHSD	KM	
20309	(20075)	+	**DR**	DR	XHSD	KM	
20310	(20190)	+	**DR**	DR	XHSD	KM	

20311	(20102)	+ **DR**	DR XHSD	KM
20312	(20042)	+ **DR**	DR XHSD	KM
20313	(20194)	+ **DR**	DR XHSD	KM
20314	(20117)	+ **DR**	DR XHSD	KM
20315	(20104)	+ **DR**	DR XHSD	KM

Class 20/9. Direct Rail Services (former Hunslet-Barclay) refurbished locos.
Details as Class 20/0 except:

Refurbished: 1989 by Hunslet-Barclay at Kilmarnock.
Train Brakes: Air.   **Fuel Capacity:** 1727 (+ 4727) litres.

20901	(20041)	**DR**	DR XHSD	KM
20902	(20060)	+ **DR**	DR XHSD	KM
20903	(20083)	+ **DR**	DR XHSD	KM
20904	(20101)	**DR**	DR XHSD	KM
20905	(20225)	+ **0**	DR XHSS	ZB (S)
20906	(20219)	**DR**	DR XHSD	KM

CLASS 31 BRUSH/ENGLISH ELECTRIC A1A-A1A

Built: 1958–62 by Brush Traction at Loughborough.
Engine: English Electric 12SVT of 1100 kW (1470 h.p.) at 850 r.p.m.
Main Generator: Brush TG160-48.   **Traction Motors:** Brush TM73-68.
Maximum Tractive Effort: 160 kN (35900 lbf).
Continuous Tractive Effort: 83 kN (18700 lbf) at 23.5 m.p.h.
Power At Rail: 872 kW (1170 h.p.).   **Train Brakes:** Air & vacuum.
Brake Force: 49 t.   **Dimensions:** 17.30 x 2.67 m.
Weight: 106.7–111 t.   **Wheel Diameter:** 1092/1003 mm.
Design Speed: 90 m.p.h.   **Maximum Speed:** 90 m.p.h.
Fuel Capacity: 2409 litres.   **RA:** 5 or 6.
Train Supply: Not equipped.   **Multiple Working:** Blue Star.

Originally numbered D 5520–5699, 5800–5862 (not in order).

Non-standard livery/numbering:

31110 carries number D5528.

Class 31/1. Standard Design. RA: 5.

31102	**CE**	E	WNZX	CE	
31105	**T**	FR	SDXL	BH	
31106	**CE**	HJ	SDXL	DF	
31107	**CE**	HJ	SDXL	BH	
31110 a	**G**	E	WMOC	OC	TRACTION magazine
31113	**CE**	E	WNXX	OM	
31128		FR	SDXL	DF	
31144	**CE**	X		CL	
31154	**CE**	E	WNYX	OM	
31190	**FR**	PO	SDFR	DF	GRYPHON
31200	**F**	E	WNZX	CW	
31203	**CE**	CR	CROL	LB	
31206	**CE**	CR	CROL	LB	
31207	**CE**	E	WNXX	OC	

31210	**FO**	CR	CROL	LB
31233	**CE**	E	WNYX	OM
31275	**F**	E	WNZX	CS
31285	**CE**	FR	SDXL	CL
31289	**B**	FR	SDXL	TM
31301	**FR**	FR	SDXL	TM
31306	**CE**	E	WNXX	OM
31308	**CE**	E	WNXX	OM
31319	**F**	E	WNZX	CW

Class 31/4. Electric Train Supply equipment. RA: 6.
Class 31/5. Train Heating Equipment isolated. RA6.

31407	**IM**	FR	SDXL	BS	
31410	**RR**	E	WNZX	CS	
31411	**DG**	FR	SDXL	BS	
31512	**CE**	X	SDXL	BS	
31514	**CE**	E	WNXX	OM	
31415		FR	SDXL	FD	
31417	**DG**	FR	SDXL	BS	
31420	**IM**	E	WNXX	OM	
31421	**RR**	E	WNZX	CW	
31422		FD	SDXL	TM	
31423		FR	SDXL	DF	
31424		FR	SDXL	BH	
31426	**CE**	FR	SDXL	DF	
31427	**B**	E	WNXX	IP	
31530	**CE**	E	WNZX	SP	
31533	**CE**	PO	SDXL	BC	
31437	**CE**	FR	SDXL	FD	
31439	**RR**	FR	SDXL	FD	
31541	**CE**	E	WNZX	OM	
31442	**B**		WNZX	CW	
31449	**B**	FR	SDXL	TM	
31452	**FR**	FR	SDFR	DF	MINOTAUR
31554	**CE**	FR	SDXL	WA	
31459	**FR**	FR	SDFR	DF	CERBERUS
31460	**B**	FR	SDXL	BC	
31461		FR	SDXL	TM	
31462		FR	SDXL	TM	
31465	**RR**	E	WNXX	OM	
31466 a	**E**	E	WNXX	OC	
31468	**FR**	FR	SDFR	DF	HYDRA

Class 31/6. ETS through wiring and controls. RA: 5.

31601	(31186)	**FR**	FR	SDFR	DF	BLETCHLEY PARK 'STATION X'
31602	(31191)	**FR**	FR	SDFR	DF	CHIMAERA

CLASS 33   BRCW/SULZER   Bo-Bo

Built: 1960–62 by the Birmingham Railway Carriage & Wagon Company at Smethwick.

Engine: Sulzer 8LDA28 of 1160 kW (1550 h.p.) at 750 r.p.m.
Main Generator: Crompton Parkinson CG391B1.
Traction Motors: Crompton Parkinson C171C2.
Maximum Tractive Effort: 200 kN (45000 lbf).
Continuous Tractive Effort: 116 kN (26000 lbf) at 17.5 m.p.h.
Power At Rail: 906 kW (1215 h.p.). **Train Brakes:** Air & vacuum.
Brake Force: 35 t.   **Dimensions:** 15.47 x 2.82 (2.64 m. 33/2).
Weight: 77.7 t.   **Wheel Diameter:** 1092 mm.
Design Speed: 85 m.p.h.   **Maximum Speed:** 85 m.p.h.
Fuel Capacity: 3410 litres.   **RA:** 6.
Train Supply: Electric, index 48 (750 V d.c. only).
Multiple Working: Blue Star.

Originally numbered in series D 6500–97 but not in order.

Non-standard numbering:

33051 also carries number 6569.
33109 also carries number D6525.
33116 also carries number D6535.
33208 carries number D6593.

Class 33/0. Standard Design.

33002	CE	DR	XHSS	KM	
33008	G	DR	XHSS	KM	
33019	CE	E	WNZX	ML	
33021	O	WF	SDFR	DF	Eastleigh
33023	B	DR	XHSS	KM	
33025	CE	E	WNZX	ML	
33026	CE	HN	WNZX	EH	
33029	B	DR	XHSS	KM	
33030	E	E	WSZX	ML	
33046	CE	E	WNZX	EH	
33051	B	HN	WNZX	EH	Shakespeare Cliff
33053	F	DR	XHSS	KM	
33057	CE	DR	XHSS	KM	

Class 33/1. Fitted with Buckeye Couplings & SR Multiple Working Equipment for use with SR EMUs, TC stock & Class 73. Also fitted with flashing light adaptor for use on Weymouth Quay line.

33103	b	G	CM	CTLO	DF	
33108	b	FR	PO	SDFR	DF	
33109	b	B	HL	HYSB	RL	Captain Bill Smith RNR
33116	b	B	E	WNZX	OM	

Class 33/2. Built to Former Loading Gauge of Tonbridge–Battle Line.
All equipped with slow speed control.

33202		CE	E	WNZX	EH
33203		F	DR	XHSS	KM
33205		F	E	WNZX	OM
33207		F	DR	XHSS	KM
33208	e*	G	HL	MBDL	RL

CLASS 37   ENGLISH ELECTRIC   Co-Co

Built: 1960–65 by English Electric Company at Vulcan Foundry, Newton le Willows or by Robert Stephenson & Hawthorn at Darlington.
Engine: English Electric 12CSVT of 1300 kW (1750 h.p.) at 850 r.p.m.
Main Generator: English Electric 822/10G.
Traction Motors: English Electric 538/A.
Maximum Tractive Effort: 245 kN (55500 lbf).
Continuous Tractive Effort: 156 kN (35000 lbf) at 13.6 m.p.h.
Power At Rail: 932 kW (1250 h.p.).   **Train Brakes:** Air & vacuum.
Brake Force: 50 t.   **Dimensions:** 18.75 x 2.74 m.
Weight: 102.8–108.4 t.   **Wheel Diameter:** 1092 mm.
Design Speed: 90 m.p.h.   **Maximum Speed:** 80 m.p.h.
Fuel Capacity: 4046 (+ 7678) litres.   **RA:** 5 (° 6).
Train Supply: Not equipped.   **Multiple Working:** Blue Star.

Originally numbered D 6600–8, 6700–6999 (not in order). 37274 is the second loco to carry that number. It was renumbered to avoid confusion with Class 37/3 locos.

Non-standard liveries/numbering:

37131 also carries number 6831.
37351 carries number 37002 on one side only.
37403 carries number D6607.
37906 is in Railfreight grey with yellow cabs, red buffer beam & solebar stripe and large double arrow logo.

Class 37/0. Standard Design. Details as above.

37010	a	CE	E	WNYX	SP
37012		CE	X	WNZX	SP
37023		ML	E	WNXX	OM	Stratford TMD Quality Approved
37029		B	RV	RTLO	CP
37037	a	F	E	WNYX	SP
37038		CE	IR	MBDL	BQ
37040		E	E	WNYX	SP
37042	+	E	E	WKAC	OC
37046	a	CE	E	WNXX	TY
37047	+	ML	E	WKAC	OC
37048		F	X		TT
37051		E	E	WKAC	OC	Merehead
37054		CE	E	WNYX	ML
37055	+	ML	E	WKAD	CD
37057	+	E	E	WKAD	CD	Viking
37058	a+	CE	E	WNXX	TY
37059	a+	F	DR	XHSS	IM
37065	+	ML	E	WKAD	CD
37068		F	DR	XHSS	IM
37069	a+	CE	DR	XHSS	SP
37071	a+	CE	E	WNYX	SP
37073	a+	F	E	WNYX	SP
37074	a+	ML	E	WNYX	SP

37077	a	**ML**	E	WNXX	TY
37088		**F**	E	WNZX	SP
37097		**CE**	E	WNYX	MH
37098		**CE**	E	WNZX	OM
37100	a	**F**	E	WNXX	TY
37109		**E**	E	WNAC	OC
37114	r+	**E**	E	WKAC	OC	City of Worcester
37116	+	**B**	E	WKAD	CD	Sister Dora
37131	+	**F**	E	WNYX	SP
37133	a	**CE**	E	WNYX	SP
37137		**?**	E	WNZX	TT
37139		**F**	E	WNZX	TT
37144		**F**	DR	XHSS	IM
37146	a	**CE**	E	WNXX	TT
37152		**I**	E	WNYX	ML
37162	+	**DG**	E	WNYX	SP
37165	a+	**CE**	E	WNYX	TT
37170	a	**CE**	E	WNYX	SP
37174	a	**E**	E	WKAC	OC
37175	a	**CE**	E	WNYX	OM
37178	+	**F**	E	WNYX	EH
37185	+	**CE**	E	WNYX	SP
37188		**CE**	E	WNZX	TT
37196	a	**CE**	E	WNXX	TY
37197			IR	MBDL	BQ
37198	+	**ML**	E	WNXX	PB
37201		**CE**	E	WNZX	BS
37203		**ML**	E	WKAC	OC
37212	+	**F**	E	WNYX	EH
37213		**F**	E	WNZX	TT
37214		**T**	E	WNZX	SP
37216	+	**ML**	E	WKAD	CD
37217	+	**B**	E	WNYX	AY
37218		**F**	DR	XHSS	IM
37219		**ML**	E	WNXX	EH
37220	+	**E**	E	WNXX	TO
37221	a	**F**	E	WNXX	TY
37223		**F**	DR	XHSS	IM
37225	+	**F**	E	WNYX	SP
37227		**F**	E	WNZX	OM
37229		**F**	E	WNZX	BW
37230	+	**CE**	E	WNYX	TT
37235		**F**	E	WNZX	DD
37238	a+	**F**	E	WNXX	TY
37240		**CE**	E	WNZX	SP
37248	+	**ML**	E	WKAM	ML	Midland Railway Centre
37250	a+	**F**	E	WNXX	TY
37261	a+	**F**	E	MBDL	BQ
37262	+	**DG**	DR	XHSS	SP	Dounreay[1]
37263		**CE**	E	WNYX	EH
37264		**CE**	E	WNZX	SP

37275	+	**B**	E	WNYX	TO
37278		**F**	E	WNZX	TT
37293	a+	**ML**	E	WNXX	TY
37294	a+	**CE**	E	WNXX	TY
37298	a+	**E**	E	WNYX	SP
37308	+	**B**	E	WMOC	OM

Class 37/3. Re-geared (CP7) bogies. Details as Class 37/0 except:

Maximum Tractive Effort: 250 kN (56180 lbf).
Continuous Tractive Effort: 184 kN (41250 lbf) at 11.4 m.p.h.
Design Speed: 80 m.p.h.

37331		**B**	HN		BH	
37334		**F**	RT		BQ	
37340		**F**	DR	XHSS	IM	
37345		**F**	E	WNZX	IM	
37350	+	**G**		MDDL	YM	
37351	+	**CE**	E	WNXX	CD	
37358	+	**F**	E	WNYX	IM	
37370	a	**E**	E	WNYX	SP	
37372		**ML**	E	WKAC	OC	
37375	a+	**ML**	E	WKAC	OC	
37376	a+	**F**	E	WNYX	SP	
37377	+	**CE**	E	WKAD	CD	
37379	a	**ML**	E	WKAM	ML	Ipswich WRD Quality Approved
37380		**F**	CR	CROL	LB	
37383	+	**ML**	RT		BQ	
37384		**CE**	DR	XHSS	SP	

Class 37/4. Refurbished with electric train supply equipment. Main generator replaced by alternator. Re-geared (CP7) bogies. Details as class 37/0 except:
Main Alternator: Brush BA1005A.   **Power At Rail:** 935 kW (1254 h.p.).
Maximum Tractive Effort: 256 kN (57440 lbf).
Continuous Tractive Effort: 184 kN (41250 lbf) at 11.4 m.p.h.
Weight: 107 t.
Design Speed: 80 m.p.h.
Fuel Capacity: 7678 (z 4046) litres.
Train Supply: Electric, index 38.

37401	r	**GS**	E	WKBM	ML	Great Scottish & Western Railway Co. The Royal Scotsman
37402		**F**	E	WNXX	CD	Bont Y Bermo
37403	ar	**G**	E	WNXX	BW	Ben Cruachan
37404		**T**	E	WNZX	SP	
37405	r	**E**	E	WKBM	ML	
37406		**F**	E	WNXX	BW	The Saltire Society
37407		**F**	E	WNXX	CD	
37408	r	**E**	E	WKCK	CF	Loch Rannoch
37409	r	**F**	E	WNXX	ML	Loch Awe
37410		**F**	E	WNXX	ML	Aluminium 100
37411	r	**E**	E	WKBM	ML	The Scottish Railway Preservation Society
37412		**F**	E	WKCK	CF	Driver John Elliott

37413 r	E	E	WNXX	DD	
37414	RR	E	WNYX	SP	Cathays C & W Works 1846–1993
37415 r	E	E	WKBM	ML	
37416 r	E	E	WKBM	ML	Sir Robert McAlpine/Concrete Bob
37417 a	E	E	WNXX	BW	
37418	E	E	WKCK	CF	East Lancashire Railway
37419	E	E	WKCK	CF	
37420	RR	E	WNXX	CD	The Scottish Hosteller
37421 r	E	E	WKBM	ML	
37422	RR	E	WNXX	BW	
37423	F	E	WNXX	ML	Sir Murray Morrison 1873–1948 Pioneer of the British Aluminium Industry
37424	F	E	WNXX	ML	
37425	RR	E	WNXX	BW	
37426	E	E	WKBM	ML	
37427 r	E	E	WKBM	ML	
37428 r	GS	E	WKBM	ML	
37429	RR	E	WNXX	ML	
37430 ar	F	E	WNXX	ML	Cwmbrân

Class 37/5. Refurbished without train supply equipment. Main generator replaced by alternator. Re-geared (CP7) bogies.
Details as Class 37/4 except:

Maximum Tractive Effort: 248 kN (55590 lbf).
Weight: 106.1–110.0 t.

37503 r§	E	E	WKAD	CD	
37505 a§	F	E	WNXX	AY	British Steel Workington
37509 a§	F	E	WKSN	TO	
37510 a	I	E	WNXX	TE	
37513 as§	LH	E	WNXX	OC	
37515 as	F	E	WNXX	TE	
37516 ss	LH	E	WNXX	TO	
37517 as§	LH	E	WKSN	TO	
37518 a§	F	E	WNXX	AY	
37519	F	E	WNYX	EH	
37520 r§	E	E	WKSN	TO	
37521 r§	E	E	WKSN	TO	English China Clays

Class 37/6. Refurbished for Nightstar services. Main generator replaced by alternator, re-geared bogies and UIC jumpers. Details as class 37/5 except:

Maximum Speed: 90 m.p.h.   **Train Brake:** Air.
Train Supply: Not equipped, but electric through wired.
Multiple Working: TDM († plus Blue Star).

37601	EP	EU	GPSV	OC	
37602	EP	EU	GPSV	OC	
37603	EP	EU	GPSV	OC	
37604	EP	EU	GPSV	OC	
37605	EP	EU	GPSV	OC	
37606	EP	EU	GPSV	OC	
37607 †	DR	DR	XHSD	KM	

37608 †	**DR**	DR	XHSD	KM	
37609 †	**DR**	DR	XHSD	KM	
37610 †	**DR**	DR	XHSD	KM	
37611 †	**DR**	DR	XHSD	KM	
37612 †	**DR**	DR	XHSD	KM	

Class 37/5 continued.

37667 rs§	**E**	E	WKSN	TO	Meldon Quarry Centenary
37668 s§	**E**	E	WKSN	TO	
37669 r§	**E**	E	WKSN	TO	
37670 r§	**E**	E	WKSN	TO	
37671 a	**F**	E	WNXX	TY	
37672 as	**F**	E	WNXX	TE	
37673 §	**F**	E	WNXX	TE	
37674 §	**F**	E	WKSN	TO	St. Blaise Church 1445–1995
37675 as§	**F**	E	WNSN	TO	Margam TMD
37676 a§	**F**	E	WNXX	TE	
37677 a§	**F**	E	WNXX	TE	
37678 a§	**F**	E	WNXX	BS	
37679 a§	**F**	E	WNXX	AY	
37680 a§	**F**	E	WNXX	TE	
37682 r§	**E**	E	WKAD	CD	Hartlepool Pipe Mill
37683 a	**F**	E	WNXX	TE	
37684 ar§	**E**	E	WKAD	CD	Peak National Park
37685 a§	**I**	E	WNSN	TO	
37686 a	**F**	E	WNYX	SP	
37688 §	**E**	E	WKAD	CD	
37689 a§	**F**	E	WKSN	TO	
37692 s§	**F**	E	WNXX	TE	
37693 as	**F**	E	WNXX	TY	
37694 §	**E**	E	WKSN	TO	
37695 s§	**E**	E	WKAD	CD	
37696 as	**F**	E	WNXX	TY	
37697 §	**E**	E	WNXX	TT	
37698 a§	**LH**	E	WKSN	TO	

Class 37/7. Refurbished locos. Main generator replaced by alternator. Re-geared (CP7) bogies. Ballast weights added. Details as class 37/5 except:
Main Alternator: GEC G564AZ (37796–803) Brush BA1005A (others).
Maximum Tractive Effort: 276 kN (62000 lbf).
Weight: 120 t.   **RA:** 7.

37701 as	**F**	E	WNXX	OM	
37702 s	**E**	E	WKGS	ES	Taff Merthyr
37703	**E**	E	WKGS	ES	
37704 s	**E**	E	WKAD	CD	
37705	**F**	E	WNXX	ML	
37706	**E**	E	WKAD	CD	
37707	**E**	E	WKAD	CD	
37708 a	**F**	E	WNXX	TY	
37709	**F**	E	WNXX	IM	
37710	**LH**	E	WKAD	CD	

37711	F	E	WNYX	TO	
37712 a	E	E	WKAC	OC	
37713	LH	E	WNXX	CD	
37714 a	E	E	WKGS	ES	
37715	F	E	WNYX	SP	
37716	E	E	WKGS	ES	
37717	E	E	WKAD	CD	Berwick Middle School
					Railsafe Trophy Winners 1998
37718	E	E	WKGS	ES	
37719 a	F	E	WNXX	OM	
37796 as	F	E	WNXX	TY	
37797 s	E	E	WKAD	CD	
37798	ML	E	WKAD	CD	
37799 as	E	E	WKGS	ES	
37800 a	E	E	WKGS	ES	
37801 s	E	E	WKGS	ES	
37802 s	E	E	WKGS	ES	
37803 a	ML	E	WNXX	TY	
37883	E	E	WKGS	ES	
37884	LH	E	WKGS	TO	
37885	E	E	WKGS	ES	
37886	E	E	WKAC	OC	Sir Dyfed/County of Dyfed
37887 s	F	E	WNXX	IM	
37888 z	E	E	WKGS	ES	
37889	F	E	WNYX	CD	
37890 a	F	E	WNXX	CD	
37891 a	F	E	WNXX	TY	
37892	F	E	WNXX	OM	Ripple Lane[1]
37893	E	E	WKGR	TO	
37894 as	F	E	WNXX	TY	
37895 s	E	E	WKGR	TO	
37896 s	F	E	WKAD	CD	
37897 s	F	E	WNXX	BS	
37898 s	F	E	WNYX	BW	Cwmbargoed DP
37899 s	E	E	WKGS	ES	

Class 37/9. Refurbished locos. New power unit. Main generator replaced by alternator.
Ballast weights added. Details as Class 37/4 except:
Engine: Mirrlees MB275T of 1340 kW (1800 h.p.) at 1000 r.p.m. (§ Ruston RK270T of 1340 kW (1800 h.p.) at 900 r.p.m.).
Train supply: Not equipped.
Main Alternator: Brush BA1005A (ç GEC G564AZ).
Maximum Tractive Effort: 279 kN (62680 lbf).
Continuous Tractive Effort: 184 kN (41250 lbf) at 11.4 m.p.h.
Weight: 120 t.   **RA:** 7.

37901	F	E	WNYX	CF	Mirrlees Pioneer
37902	F	E	WNYX	IM	
37903	F	E	WNYX	CD	
37905 §s	F	E	WMOC	OC	
37906 §s	0	E	WMOC	OC	

CLASS 43   BREL/PAXMAN   Bo-Bo

Built: 1976–82 by BREL at Crewe Works.
Engine: Paxman Valenta 12RP200L of 1680 kW (2250 h.p.) at 1500 r.p.m.
(* Paxman 12VP185 of 2010 kW (2700 h.p.) at 1800 r.p.m.).
Main Alternator: Brush BA1001B.
Traction Motors: Brush TMH68–46 or GEC G417AZ, frame mounted.
Maximum Tractive Effort: 80 kN (17980 lbf).
Continuous Tractive Effort: 46 kN (10340 lbf) at 64.5 m.p.h.
Power At Rail: 1320 kW (1770 h.p.).   **Train Brakes:** Air.
Brake Force: 35 t.   **Dimensions:** 17.79 x 2.71 m.
Weight: 70 t.   **Wheel Diameter:** 1020 mm.
Design Speed: 125 m.p.h.   **Maximum Speed:** 125 m.p.h.
Fuel Capacity: 4500 litres.   **RA:** 5.
Train Supply: Three-phase electric.
Multiple Working: Within class, jumpers at non-driving end only.

43002	FG	A	IWRP	PM	TECHNIQUEST
43003	FW	A	IWRP	PM	
43004	FG	A	IWRP	PM	Borough of Swindon
43005	FG	A	IWRP	PM	
43006	V	A	IWCP	LA	
43007	V	A	IWCP	LA	
43008	V	A	IWCP	LA	
43009	FG	A	IWRP	PM	
43010	FG	A	IWRP	PM	
43011	FG	A	SCXL	ZC (S)	Reader 125
43012	FG	A	IWRP	PM	
43013	V	P	ICCP	LA	
43014	V	P	ICCP	LA	
43015	FG	A	IWRP	PM	
43016	FG	A	IWRP	PM	
43017	FG	A	IWRP	LA	
43018	FG	A	IWRP	LA	The Red Cross
43019	FG	A	IWRP	LA	Dinas Abertawe/City of Swansea
43020	FG	A	IWRP	LA	John Grooms
43021	FG	A	IWRP	LA	
43022	FG	A	IWRP	LA	
43023	FG	A	IWRP	LA	County of Cornwall
43024	FG	A	IWRP	LA	
43025	FG	A	IWRP	LA	Exeter
43026	FG	A	IWRP	LA	City of Westminster
43027	FG	A	IWRP	LA	Glorious Devon
43028	FG	A	IWRP	LA	
43029	FW	A	IWRP	LA	
43030	FG	A	IWRP	PM	Christian Lewis Trust
43031	FG	A	IWRP	PM	
43032	FW	A	IWRP	PM	The Royal Regiment of Wales
43033	FG	A	IWRP	PM	
43034	FG	A	IWRP	PM	The Black Horse

43035	FG	A	IWRP	PM	
43036	FG	A	IWRP	PM	
43037	FG	A	IWRP	PM	
43038	GN	A	IECP	EC	
43039	GN	A	IECP	EC	
43040	FG	A	IWRP	PM	
43041	FG	A	IWRP	LA	City of Discovery
43042	FG	A	IWRP	LA	
43043	MM	P	IMLP	NL	LEICESTERSHIRE COUNTY CRICKET CLUB
43044	MM	P	IMLP	NL	Borough of Kettering
43045	MM	P	IMLP	NL	
43046	MM	P	IMLP	NL	Royal Philharmonic
43047 *	MM	P	IMLP	NL	
43048	MM	P	IMLP	NL	
43049	MM	P	IMLP	NL	Neville Hill
43050	MM	P	IMLP	NL	
43051	MM	P	IMLP	NL	
43052	MM	P	IMLP	NL	
43053	MM	P	IMLP	NL	Leeds United
43054	MM	P	IMLP	NL	
43055	MM	P	IMLP	NL	Sheffield Star
43056	MM	P	IMLP	NL	
43057	MM	P	IMLP	NL	
43058	MM	P	IMLP	NL	MIDLAND PRIDE
43059 *	MM	P	IMLP	NL	
43060	MM	P	IMLP	NL	County of Leicestershire
43061	MM	P	IMLP	NL	
43062	V	P	ICCP	LA	
43063	V	P	ICCP	LA	Maiden Voyager
43064	MM	P	IMLP	NL	
43065	V	P	ICCP	LA	
43066	MM	P	IMLP	NL	Nottingham Playhouse
43067	V	P	ICCP	LA	
43068	V	P	ICCP	LA	The Red Arrows
43069	V	P	ICCP	LA	
43070	V	P	ICCP	LA	
43071	V	P	ICCP	LA	Forward Birmingham
43072	MM	P	IMLP	NL	Derby Etches Park
43073	MM	P	IMLP	NL	
43074 *	MM	P	IMLP	NL	BBC EAST MIDLANDS TODAY
43075 *	MM	P	IMLP	NL	
43076	MM	P	IMLP	NL	THE MASTER CUTLER 1947–1997
43077	MM	P	IMLP	NL	
43078	V	P	ICCP	LA	Golowan Festival Penzance
43079	V	P	ICCP	LA	
43080	V	P	ICCP	LA	
43081	MM	P	IMLP	NL	
43082	MM	P	IMLP	NL	DERBYSHIRE FIRST
43083	MM	P	IMLP	NL	
43084	V	P	ICCP	LA	County of Derbyshire

43085	MM	P	IMLP	NL	
43086	V	P	ICCP	LA	
43087	V	P	ICCP	LA	
43088	V	P	ICCP	LA	
43089	V	P	ICCP	LA	
43090	V	P	ICCP	LA	
43091	V	P	ICCP	LA	
43092	V	P	ICCP	LA	Institution of Mechanical Engineers
43093	V	P	ICCP	LA	Lady in Red
43094	V	P	ICCP	LA	
43095	GN	A	IECP	EC	
43096	GN	A	IECP	EC	
43097	V	P	ICCP	LA	
43098	V	P	ICCP	LA	railwaychildren
43099	V	P	ICCP	LA	
43100	V	P	ICCP	LA	
43101	V	P	ICCP	LA	
43102	V	P	ICCP	LA	
43103	V	P	ICCP	LA	
43104	V	A	IWCP	LA	City of Edinburgh
43105	GN	A	IECP	EC	City of Inverness
43106	GN	A	IECP	EC	
43107	GN	A	IECP	EC	
43108	GN	A	IECP	EC	Old Course St Andrews
43109	GN	A	IECP	EC	
43110	GN	A	IECP	EC	
43111	GN	A	IECP	EC	
43112	GN	A	IECP	EC	Doncaster
43113	GN	A	IECP	EC	
43114	GN	A	IECP	EC	
43115	GN	A	IECP	EC	
43116	GN	A	IECP	EC	
43117	GN	A	IECP	EC	
43118	GN	A	IECP	EC	
43119	GN	A	IECP	EC	
43120	GN	A	IECP	EC	
43121	V	P	ICCP	LA	
43122	V	P	ICCP	LA	South Yorkshire Metropolitan County
43123	V	P	ICCP	LA	
43124	FG	A	IWRP	PM	
43125	FG	A	IWRP	PM	Merchant Venturer
43126	FG	A	IWRP	PM	City of Bristol
43127	FG	A	IWRP	PM	
43128	FG	A	IWRP	PM	
43129	FG	A	IWRP	PM	
43130	FG	A	IWRP	PM	Sulis Minerva
43131	FG	A	IWRP	PM	Sir Felix Pole
43132	FG	A	IWRP	PM	
43133	FG	A	IWRP	PM	
43134	FG	A	IWRP	PM	County of Somerset

43135	**FG**	A	IWRP	PM	
43136	**FG**	A	IWRP	PM	
43137	**FG**	A	IWRP	PM	Newton Abbot 150
43138	**FG**	A	IWRP	PM	
43139	**FG**	A	IWRP	PM	
43140	**FG**	A	IWRP	PM	
43141	**FG**	A	IWRP	PM	
43142	**FG**	A	IWRP	PM	
43143	**FG**	A	IWRP	PM	
43144	**FG**	A	IWRP	PM	
43145	**FG**	A	IWRP	PM	
43146	**FG**	A	IWRP	PM	
43147	**FG**	A	IWRP	PM	
43148	**FG**	A	IWRP	PM	
43149	**FG**	A	IWRP	PM	B.B.C. Wales Today
43150	**FG**	A	IWRP	PM	Bristol Evening Post
43151	**FG**	A	IWRP	PM	
43152	**FG**	A	IWRP	PM	
43153	**V**	P	ICCP	LA	THE ENGLISH RIVIERA TORQUAY PAIGNTON BRIXHAM
43154	**V**	P	ICCP	LA	INTERCITY
43155	**V**	P	ICCP	LA	City of Aberdeen
43156	**V**	P	ICCP	LA	
43157	**V**	P	ICCP	LA	
43158	**V**	P	ICCP	LA	Dartmoor The Pony Express
43159	**V**	P	ICCP	LA	
43160	**V**	P	ICCP	LA	
43161	**V**	P	ICCP	LA	
43162	**V**	P	ICCP	LA	
43163	**FG**	A	IWRP	LA	
43164	**FG**	A	IWRP	LA	
43165	**FG**	A	IWRP	LA	
43166	**V**	A	IWCP	LA	
43167	**GN**	A	IECP	EC	
43168 *	**FG**	A	IWRP	LA	
43169 *	**FG**	A	IWRP	LA	The National Trust
43170 *	**FG**	A	IWRP	LA	Edward Paxman
43171	**FG**	A	IWRP	LA	
43172	**FG**	A	IWRP	LA	
43174	**FG**	A	IWRP	LA	Bristol–Bordeaux
43175 *	**FG**	A	IWRP	LA	
43176	**FG**	A	IWRP	LA	
43177 *	**FG**	A	IWRP	LA	University of Exeter
43178	**V**	A	IWCP	LA	
43179 *	**FG**	A	IWRP	LA	Pride of Laira
43180	**V**	P	ICCP	LA	City of Newcastle upon Tyne
43181	**FG**	A	IWRP	LA	Devonport Royal Dockyard 1693–1993
43182	**FG**	A	IWRP	LA	
43183	**FG**	A	IWRP	LA	
43184	**V**	A	IWCP	LA	

43185	FG	A	IWRP	LA	Great Western
43186	FG	A	IWRP	LA	Sir Francis Drake
43187	FG	A	IWRP	LA	
43188	FG	A	IWRP	LA	City of Plymouth
43189	FG	A	IWRP	LA	RAILWAY HERITAGE TRUST
43190	FG	A	IWRP	LA	
43191 *	FG	A	IWRP	LA	Seahawk
43192	FG	A	IWRP	LA	City of Truro
43193	V	P	ICCP	LA	Plymouth SPIRIT OF DISCOVERY
43194	V	P	ICCP	LA	
43195	V	P	ICCP	LA	British Red Cross 125th Birthday 1995[1]
43196	V	P	ICCP	LA	The Newspaper Society Founded 1836
43197	V	P	ICCP	LA	The RAILWAY MAGAZINE
43198	V	P	ICCP	LA	HMS Penzance

CLASS 45   BR/SULZER   1Co-Co1

Built: 1963 by BR at Derby Locomotive Works.
Engine: Sulzer 12LDA28B of 1860 kW (2500 h.p.) at 750 r.p.m.
Main Generator: Crompton-Parkinson CG426 A1.
Traction Motors: Crompton-Parkinson C172 A1.
Maximum Tractive Effort: 245 kN (55000 lbf).
Continuous Tractive Effort: 134 kN (31600 lbf) at 22.3 m.p.h.
Power At Rail: 1490 kW (2000 h.p.).   **Train Brakes:** Air & vacuum.
Brake Force: 63 t.   **Dimensions:** 20.70 x 2.78 m.
Weight: 140 t.   **Wheel Diameter:** 914/1143 mm.
Design Speed: 90 m.p.h.   **Maximum Speed:** 90 m.p.h.
Fuel Capacity: 3591 litres.   **RA:** 7.
Train Supply: Electric.   **Multiple Working:** Not equipped.

Originally numbered D 61.

| 45015 | B | E | WNZX | TT | |
| 45112 | FR | FR | SDMS | DF | THE ROYAL ARMY ORDNANCE CORPS |

CLASS 46   BR/SULZER   1Co-Co1

Built: 1963 by BR at Derby Locomotive Works.
Engine: Sulzer 12LDA28B of 1860 kW (2500 h.p.) at 750 r.p.m.
Main Generator: Brush TG160-60.   **Traction Motors:** Brush TM73-68 Mk3.
Maximum Tractive Effort: 245 kN (55000 lbf).
Continuous Tractive Effort: 141 kN (31600 lbf) at 22.3 m.p.h.
Power At Rail: 1460 kW (1960 h.p.).   **Train Brakes:** Air & vacuum.
Brake Force: 63 t.   **Dimensions:** 20.70 x 2.78 m.
Weight: 140 t.   **Wheel Diameter:** 914/1143 mm.
Design Speed: 90 m.p.h.   **Maximum Speed:** 75 m.p.h.
Fuel Capacity: 3591 litres.   **RA:** 7.
Train Supply: Not equipped.   **Multiple Working:** Not equipped.

Non-standard livery/numbering: Carries original number D 172.

| 46035 | G | CN | MBDL | CQ | Ixion |

CLASS 47   BR/BRUSH/SULZER   Co-Co

Built: 1963–67 by Brush Traction, at Loughborough or by BR at Crewe Works.
Engine: Sulzer 12LDA28C of 1920 kW(*1785 kW) (2580 (*2400) h.p.) at 750 r.p.m.
Main Generator: Brush TG160-60 Mk4 or TM172-50 Mk1.
Traction Motors: Brush TM64-68 Mk1 or Mk1A.
Maximum Tractive Effort: 267 kN (60000 lbf).
Continuous Tractive Effort: 133 kN (30000 lbf) at 26 m.p.h.
Power At Rail: 1550 kW (2080 h.p.).   **Train Brakes:** Air.
Brake Force: 61 t.   **Dimensions:** 19.38 x 2.79 m.
Weight: 111.5–120.6 t.   **Wheel Diameter:** 1143 mm.
Design Speed: 95 m.p.h.   **Maximum Speed:** 75 m.p.h.
Fuel Capacity: 3273 (+ 5550; †4410 litres).
Train Supply: Not equipped.
Multiple Working: Green Circle (n – not equipped).

Originally numbered in series D 1100–11, 1500–1999 not in order.

Note: DFFT locos have "Dock Mode" slow speed traction control system for working trains from Felixstowe North Container Terminal.

Non-standard liveries/numbering:
47004 carries number D1524.
47114 is as **GG**, but with Freightliner logos.
47145 is dark blue with Railfreight Distribution logos.
47515 is livery **IM** on one side and all-over white on the other side.
47519 also carries number D1102.

Class 47/0 (Dual braked locos) or Class 47/2 (Air braked locos). Standard Design. Details as above.

47004	xn	**GG**	E	WMOC	OC
47033			E	WNZX	SP
47052	*	**FF**	P	DHLT	CG
47053	+	**FE**	EF	WNZX	HM
47095	+	**FE**	EF	WNYX	AN
47114	*+	**0**	FL	DHLT	CD	Freightlinerbulk
47125		**FE**	E	WNZX	SP
47145	+	**0**	GB	GBXX	BA	MERDDIN EMRYS
47146	+	**FE**	EF	WNYX	SP
47150	*+	**FL**	FL	DFLM	CD
47152	*+	**FF**	FL	DHLT	SZ
47156		**F**	E	WNZX	CW
47157	*+	**FF**	P	DHLT	BA	Johnson Stevens Agencies
47186	+	**FE**	EF	WNYX	HM
47188	+	**FE**	EF	WNYX	CD
47193	n*	**FL**	P	DHLT	CG
47194		**F**	PO	SDXL	SP
47197	dn*	**FF**	P	DFFT	CD
47200	*+	**FE**	EF	WNYX	HM
47201	*+	**FE**	EF	WNZX	HM

47205 *+	**FF**	FL	DHLT	SZ	
47206 n*	**FF**	P	DFLT	CD	The Morris Dancer
47207 *+	**FF**	P	DHLT	SZ	The Felixstowe Partnership
47209 *+	**FF**	P	DHLT	CG	
47211 +	**F**	EF	WNYX	EH	
47212 xn*	**FF**	P	DFLT	CD	
47213 +	**F**	GB	GBZZ	BA	
47217 +	**FE**	EF	WNYX	SP	
47218 +	**FE**	EF	WNYX	SP	
47219 +	**FE**	EF	WNZX	HM	
47221 xn†	**F**	E	WNZX	LB	
47223	**F**	E	WNZX	SP	
47224 xn*	**F**	P	DFLT	CD	
47225 n*	**FF**	P	DHLT	CG	
47226 +	**F**	EF	WNZX	HM	
47228 +	**FE**	EF	WNYX	HM	
47229 +	**F**	EF	WNZX	HM	
47234 *+	**FF**	P	DHLT	BA	
47236 +	**FE**	FR	SDXL	SP	
47237 +	**FE**	EF	WNYX	HM	
47238	**F**	E	WNZX	BS	
47241 +	**FE**	EF	WNYX	SP	
47245 +	**FE**	EF	WNZX	DD	
47256 xn	**F**	E	WNYX	DD	
47258 *+	**FL**	FL	DFLM	CD	Forth Ports Tilbury
47270 dn*	**FF**	P	DFFT	CD	Cory Brothers 1842–1992
47279 *+	**FF**	P	DFLM	CD	
47280 +	**F**	EF	WNYX	HM	
47283 n*	**FF**	FL	DHLT	SZ	
47285 +	**FE**	EF	WNYX	TT	
47287 *+	**F**	FL	DFLM	CD	
47289 *+	**FF**	P	DFLM	CD	
47290 *+	**FF**	FL	DHLT	CG	
47292 *+	**F**	P	DFLM	CD	
47293 +	**FE**	EF	WNZX	HM	
47294	**F**	E	WNZX	TT	
47295 adn*	**F**	FL	DFFT	CD	
47296 xn*	**FF**	P	DHLT	SZ	
47297	**FE**	E	WNZX	SP	
47298 +	**F**	EF	WNYX	HM	

Class 47/3 (Dual braked locos) or Class 47/2 (Air braked locos).
Details as Class 47/0 except:
Weight: 113.7 t.

47300	**CE**	E	WNZX	SP	
47301 *+	**FF**	P	DHLT	SP	Freightliner Birmingham
47302 *+	**FF**	FL	DFLM	CD	
47303 *+	**FF**	P	DHLT	CE	Freightliner Cleveland
47305 n*	**FF**	P	DHLT	CG	
47306 +	**FE**	EF	WMOC	CG	The Sapper
47307 +	**FE**	EF	WNYX	HM	

47308 *	FF	FL	DHLT	CG	
47309 d*+	FF	FL	DFFT	CD	European Rail Operator of The Year
47310 +	FE	EF	WNYX	HM	
47312 +	FE	EF	WNYX	SP	
47313 +	F	EF	WNZX	HM	
47314 +	F	EF	WNZX	HM	
47316 +	FE	EF	WNZX	TT	
47323 d*+	FF	P	DHLT	CD	
47326 +	FE	EF	WNYX	CD	Saltley Depot Quality Approved
47328 +	F	EF	WNYX	SP	
47330 *+	FF	FL	DHLT	BA	
47331 xns	CE	E	WNYX	SP	
47334 n*	FF	P	DHLT	SZ	P & O Nedlloyd
47335 +	F	EF	WNYX	HM	
47337 *+	FF	FL	DHLT	CG	
47338 +	FE	EF	WNYX	CD	
47339 n*	FF	P	DHLT	CG	
47341	CE	E	WNZX	TT	
47344	FE	E	WNZX	SP	
47345 n*	FF	P	DHLT	CD	
47348 +	FE	EF	WNYX	IP	St. Christopher's Railway Home
47349 xn*	FF	P	DFLT	CD	
47353 n*	FF	FL	DHLT	CG	
47354 *	FF	FL	DHLT	CG	
47355	F	FR	SDXL	HM	
47358 *+	FF	P	DHLT	CD	
47360 +	FE	EF	WNZX	HM	
47361 *+	FF	P	DHLT	SZ	
47363	F	FR	SDXL	SP	
47365 +	FE	EF	WNZX	CF	Diamond Jubilee
47367 *+	FF	P	DHLT	DF	
47368 xn	F	FR	SDXL	SP	
47370 *+	FF	P	DFLM	CD	Andrew A Hodgkinson
47371 n*	FF	P	DHLT	BA	
47372 n*	FF	P	DHLT	CP	
47375 +	FE	EF	WNZX	HM	
47376 xn*	FF	P	DFLT	CD	Freightliner 1995
47377 n*	FF	P	DHLT	BA	

Class 47/4. Electric Train Supply equipment. Details as Class 47/0 except:
Weight: 120.4–125.1 t.   **Maximum Speed:** 95 m.p.h.
Fuel Capacity: 3273 (+ 5887) litres.   **RA:** 7.
Train Supply: Electric. ETH 66.
Multiple Working: Not equipped (m – Green Circle).

47462 x	RG	E	WNYX	TT	
47471 x	IM	E	WNYX	CW	
47474 x	RG	E	WNYX	SP	Sir Rowland Hill
47475 x	RX	E	WNYX	HM	
47476 x	RG	E	WNYX	TT	
47478 x	B	E	WNZX	SP	
47481 x	BL	E	WNZX	CW	

47484	x	GW	AT		CD	
47488	x	GG	FR	SDFR	DF	
47489	x	RG	FR	SDXL	SP	
47492	x	RX	E	WNYX	OO	
47501	x	RG	PO	SDXL	CD	Craftsman[1]
47513	x	BL	E	WNYX	SP	
47515	x	O	E	WNZX	CW	
47519	x+	GG	E	WNYX	CD	
47524	x	RX	E	WNYX	CW	
47525	x	FE	FR	SDXL	SP	
47526	x	BL	FR	SDXL	SP	
47528	x	IM	E	WNYX	HM	
47535	x	RX	E	WNYX	OC	
47536	x	RX	E	WNYX	SP	
47539	x	RX	E	WNZX	CW	
47540	xm	CE	E	WNYX	CW	The Institution of Civil Engineers
47547		N	E	WNYX	CD	
47550	x	IM	E	WNZX	IM	
47565	x	RX	E	WNZX	SP	
47566	x	RX	E	WNYX	SP	
47574	x	RG	E	WNYX	CD	
47575	x	RG	E	WMOC	OC	City of Hereford
47576	x	RX	E	WNYX	SP	
47596	x	RX	E	WNYX	CD	
47624	x	RX	E	WNYX	AN	
47628	x	RX	FR	SDXL	CW	
47634	x	RG	E	WNXX	SY	Holbeck
47635	x	RG	E	WHDD	CD	
47640	j	RG	E	WNYX	CD	University of Strathclyde

Class 47/7. Fitted with an older form of TDM.
Details as Class 47/4 except:
Weight: 118.7 t.**Fuel Capacity:** 5887 litres.

47701	x	FR	WF	SDFR	DF	Waverley
47702	x	V	E	WNYX	TO	County of Suffolk
47703	x	FR	FR	SDFR	DF	HERMES
47704	x	RX	FR	SDXL	CD	
47705	x	LW	P	SBXL	LB	GUY FAWKES
47707	x	RX	FR	SDXL	CW	Holyrood
47709	x	FR	FR	SDFR	DF	DIONESYS
47710	x	FR	FR	SDFR	DF	
47711	x	V	E	WNYX	TO	County of Hertfordshire
47712	x	FR	FR	SDFR	DF	ARTEMIS
47714	x	RX	E	WNZX	CW	
47715		N	FR	SDXL	CW	
47716	x	RX	E	WNZX	CW	
47717	x	RG	FR	SDXL	CW	

Class 47/7. Railnet dedicated locos. All have twin fuel tanks and are fitted with
RCH jumper cables for operating with propelling control vehicles (PCVs).

47721		RX	E	WHTN	TO	Saint Bede

47722	V	E	ILRA	TO	The Queen Mother
47725	RX	E	WHCD	CD	Bristol Barton Hill
47726	RX	E	WHTN	TO	Manchester Airport Progress
47727	RX	E	WHCD	CD	Duke of Edinburgh's Award
47732 x	RX	E	WHDD	CD	Restormel
47733	RX	E	WHTN	TO	Eastern Star
47734	RX	E	WHTN	TO	Crewe Diesel Depot Quality Approved
47736	RX	E	WHTN	TO	Cambridge Traction & Rolling Stock Depot
47737	RX	E	WHCD	CD	Resurgent
47738	RX	E	WNYX	SP	
47739	RX	E	WHCD	CD	Resourceful
47741	V	E	ILRA	TO	Resilient
47742	RX	E	WNWX	TO	The Enterprising Scot
47744	E	E	WHCD	CD	Royal Mail Cheltenham
47745 x	RX	E	WNYX	TT	Royal London Society for the Blind
47746	RX	E	WHCD	CD	The Bobby
47747	V	E	ILRA	TO	Graham Farish
47749	RX	E	WHCD	CD	Atlantic College
47750	V	E	ILRA	TO	ATLAS
47756	RX	E	WHDD	CD	Royal Mail Tyneside
47757	RX	E	WHCD	CD	Restitution
47758	E	E	WHCD	CD	
47759	RX	E	WHCD	CD	
47760	E	E	WHTN	TO	Ribblehead Viaduct
47761	RX	E	WHCD	CD	
47762	RX	E	WNXX	CD	
47763	RX	E	WNXX	ML	
47764	RX	E	WNYX	CD	Resounding
47765 x	RX	E	WNXX	BK	
47766 x	RX	E	WNXX	TT	Resolute
47767	RX	E	WHCD	CD	Saint Columba
47768 x	RX	E	WNXX	CD	
47769	V	E	WNWX	TO	Resolve
47770	RX	E	WHDD	CD	Reserved
47771	RX	E	WNXX	CD	Heaton Traincare Depot
47772 x	RX	E	WHDD	CD	
47773	RX	E	WHCM	ML	Reservist
47774 x	RX	E	WHDD	CD	Poste Restante
47775 x	RX	E	WNXX	CD	Respite
47776 x	RX	E	WHDD	CD	Respected
47777 x	RX	E	WNXX	TT	
47778	RX	E	WHCD	CD	Irresistible
47779	RX	E	WNXX	CD	
47780	RX	E	WHCD	CD	
47781	RX	E	WHCD	CD	Isle of Iona
47782	RX	E	WHCD	CD	
47783	RX	E	WHCD	CD	Saint Peter
47784	RX	E	WHCD	CD	Condover Hall
47785	E	E	WHCD	CD	Fiona Castle
47786	E	E	WHCD	CD	Roy Castle OBE
47787	RX	E	WHCD	CD	Victim Support

47789	**RX**	E	WHCD	CD	Lindisfarne
47790	**RX**	E	WHCM	ML	Dewi Sant/Saint David
47791	**RX**	E	WHCM	ML	
47792	**RX**	E	WHTN	TO	Saint Cuthbert
47793	**RX**	E	WHCD	CD	Saint Augustine

Class 47/4 continued. RA6. Max. Speed 95 m.p.h.

47798	**RP**	E	WHRD	CD	Prince William
47799	**RP**	E	WHRD	CD	Prince Henry
47802 +	**I**	AT		CD	
47805 +	**V**	P	ILRA	TO	
47806 +	**V**	P	ILRA	TO	
47807 +	**V**	P	ILRA	TO	The Lion of Vienna
47810 +	**V**	P	ILRA	TO	PORTERBROOK
47811 +	**GL**	P	IWLA	LE	
47812 +	**V**	P	ILRA	TO	
47813 +	**GL**	P	IWLA	LE	S.S. Great Britain
47814 +	**V**	P	ILRA	TO	Totnes Castle
47815 +	**GL**	P	IWLA	LE	Abertawe Landore
47816 +	**GL**	P	IWLA	LE	Bristol Bath Road Quality Approved
47817 +	**V**	P	ILRA	TO	The Institution of Mechanical Engineers
47818 +	**V**	P	ILRA	TO	Strathclyde
47822 +	**V**	P	ILRA	TO	Pride of Shrewsbury
47826 +	**I**	P	ILRA	TO	Springburn
47827 +	**V**	P	ILRA	TO	
47828 +	**V**	P	ILRA	TO	Severn Valley Railway Kidderminster Bridgnorth Bewdley
47829 +	**V**	P	ILRA	TO	
47830 +	**GL**	P	IWLA	LE	
47831 +	**V**	P	ILRA	TO	Bolton Wanderer
47832 +	**GL**	P	IWLA	LE	Tamar
47839 +	**V**	P	ILRA	TO	
47840 +	**V**	P	ILRA	TO	NORTH STAR
47841 +	**V**	P	ILRA	TO	Spirit of Chester
47843 +	**V**	P	ILRA	TO	VULCAN
47844 +	**V**	P	ILRA	TO	
47845 +	**V**	P	ILRA	LB	County of Kent
47846 +	**GL**	P	IWLA	LE	THOR
47847 +	**BL**	P	ILRA	TO	
47848 +	**V**	P	ILRA	TO	Newton Abbot Festival of Transport
47849 +	**V**	P	ILRA	TO	Cadeirlan Bangor Cathedral
47851 +	**GG**	P	ILRA	TO	
47853 +	**V**	P	ILRA	TO	
47854 +	**V**	P	ILRA	TO	Women's Royal Voluntary Service
47971	**BL**	E	WNZX	ZC	
47972	**0**	FR	SDFR	CW	

CLASS 50   ENGLISH ELECTRIC   Co-Co

Built: 1967–68 by English Electric at Vulcan Foundry, Newton-le-Willows.
Engine: English Electric 16CVST of 2010 kW (2700 h.p.) at 850 r.p.m.
Main Generator: English Electric 840/4B.
Traction Motors: English Electric 538/5A.
Maximum Tractive Effort: 216 kN (48500 lbf).
Continuous Tractive Effort: 147 kN (33000 lbf) at 23.5 m.p.h.
Power At Rail: 1540 kW (2070 h.p.).   **Train Brakes:** Air & vacuum.
Brake Force: 59 t.   **Dimensions:** 20.88 x 2.78 m.
Weight: 116.9 t.   **Wheel Diameter:** 1092 mm.
Design Speed: 105 m.p.h.   **Maximum Speed:** 90 (* 100) m.p.h.
Fuel Capacity: 4796 litres.   **RA:** 6.
Train Supply: Electric, index 66.   **Multiple Working:** Orange Square.

Originally numbered D 416–49, 400.

Non-standard livery/numbering:

50017 is "LMS Coronation Scot" style maroon with four gold bands.
50031 carries number D431.
50044 carries number D444.
50049 carries number D449.

50017	* 0	JK	MBDL	TM	
50031	B	50	MBDL	OC	
50044	B	50	MBDL	KR	
50049	B	PD	MBDL	KR	
50050	BL	HS	SDFR	BH	Fearless

CLASS 55   ENGLISH ELECTRIC   Co-Co

Built: 1961 by English Electric at Vulcan Foundry, Newton-le-Willows.
Engine: Two Napier-Deltic D18-25 of 1230 kW (1650 h.p.) each at 1500 r.p.m.
Main Generators: Two English Electric 829.
Traction Motors: English Electric 538/A.
Maximum Tractive Effort: 222 kN (50000 lbf).
Continuous Tractive Effort: 136 kN (30500 lbf) at 32.5 m.p.h.
Power At Rail: 1969 kW (2640 h.p.)   **Train Brakes:** Air & vacuum.
Brake Force: 51 t.   **Dimensions:** 21.18 x 2.68 m.
Weight: 104.7 t.   **Wheel Diameter:** 1092 mm.
Design Speed: 105 m.p.h.   **Maximum Speed:** 100 m.p.h.
Fuel Capacity: 3755 litres.   **RA:** 5.
Train Supply: Electric, index 66.   **Multiple Working:** Not equipped.

Originally numbered D 9009–19, 9000.

Non-standard numbering:

55009 carries number D9009.
55022 carries number D9000.

55009	GG	DP	MBDL	BH	ALYCIDON
55016	P	P	SBXL	TM	GORDON HIGHLANDER

| 55019 | **B** | DP | MBDL | BH | ROYAL HIGHLAND FUSILIER |
| 55022 | **GG** | 90 | SDFR | DF | ROYAL SCOTS GREY |

CLASS 56   BRUSH/BR/PAXMAN   Co-Co

Built: 1976–84 by Electroputere at Craiova, Romania (as sub contractors for Brush) or BREL at Doncaster or Crewe Works.
Engine: Ruston Paxman 16RK3CT of 2460 kW (3250 h.p.) at 900 r.p.m.
Main Alternator: Brush BA1101A.
Traction Motors: Brush TM73-62.
Maximum Tractive Effort: 275 kN (61800 lbf).
Continuous Tractive Effort: 240 kN (53950 lbf) at 16.8 m.p.h.
Power At Rail: 1790 kW (2400 h.p.).   **Train Brakes:** Air.
Brake Force: 60 t.   **Dimensions:** 19.36 x 2.79 m.
Weight: 125.2 t.   **Wheel Diameter:** 1143 mm.
Design Speed: 80 m.p.h.   **Maximum Speed:** 80 m.p.h.
Fuel Capacity: 5228 litres.   **RA:** 7.
Train Supply: Not equipped.   **Multiple Working:** Red Diamond.
Note: All equipped with Slow Speed Control.

Non-standard liveries:

56019 is in Railfreight grey with yellow cabs, red buffer beam & solebar stripe and large double arrow logo.
56063 is as **F**, but with the light grey replaced by a darker grey.

56003	**LH**	E	WNXX	DD	
56004	**B**	E	WMOC	OC	
56006	**B**	E	WMOC	OC	
56007	**F**	E	WGAI	IM	
56010	**F**	E	WNYX	DD	
56011	**E**	E	WNXX	IM	
56018	**E**	E	WGAI	IM	
56019	**O**	E	WNYX	IM	
56021	**LH**	E	WNXX	IM	
56022	**F**	E	WNXX	IM	
56025	**F**	E	WGAT	TE	
56027	**LH**	E	WGAT	TE	
56029	**F**	E	WNYX	CF	
56031	**CE**	E	WGAI	IM	
56032	**E**	E	WGAI	IM	
56033	**F**	E	WGAI	IM	Shotton Paper Mill
56034	**LH**	E	WNYX	TT	Castell Ogwr/Ogmore Castle
56036	**CE**	E	WNXX	CT	
56037	**E**	E	WGAT	TE	
56038	**E**	E	WGAT	TE	
56039	**LH**	E	WNYX	TE	
56040	**F**	E	WNXX	IM	
56041	**E**	E	WGAI	IM	
56043	**F**	E	WNXX	CT	
56044	**F**	E	WNYX	IM	Cardiff Canton Quality Approved
56045	**LH**	E	WNYX	IM	British Steel Shelton

56046	CE	E	WGAT	TE	
56047	CE	E	WNYX	IM	
56048	CE	E	WGAT	TE	
56049	CE	E	WGAT	TE	
56050	LH	E	WNYX	DD	British Steel Teesside
56051	E	E	WGAT	TE	
56052	F	E	WNXX	IM	
56053	F	E	WNXX	DD	
56054	F	E	WGAT	TE	British Steel Llanwern
56055	LH	E	WGAT	TE	
56056	F	E	WGAT	TE	
56057	E	E	WNYX	IM	British Fuels
56058	E	E	WGAT	TE	
56059	E	E	WGAI	IM	
56060	E	E	WGAT	TE	
56061	F	E	WNYX	TT	
56062	E	E	WGAI	IM	
56063	O	E	WGAT	TE	
56064	F	E	WNXX	CT	
56065	E	E	WGAT	TE	
56066	F	E	WNXX	SP	
56067	E	E	WGAT	TE	
56068	E	E	WGAT	TE	
56069	E	E	WGAI	IM	Wolverhampton Steel Terminal
56070	F	E	WGAI	IM	
56071	E	E	WGAT	TE	
56072	F	E	WGAI	IM	
56073	F	E	WGAT	TE	Tremorfa Steelworks
56074	LH	E	WGAI	IM	Kellingley Colliery
56075	F	E	WNYX	TT	
56076	F	E	WNXX	IM	
56077	LH	E	WGAT	TE	
56078	F	E	WGAI	IM	
56079	F	E	WNXX	IM	
56080	F	X		SP	Selby Coalfield
56081	E	E	WGAI	IM	
56082	F	E	WNXX	IM	
56083	LH	E	WNXX	CF	
56084	LH	E	WNXX	IM	
56085	LH	E	WGAT	TE	
56086	F	E	WNXX	IM	The Magistrates' Association
56087	E	E	WGAI	IM	ABP Port of Hull
56088	E	E	WGAI	IM	
56089	E	E	WGAT	TE	
56090	LH	E	WGAI	IM	
56091	E	E	WGAI	IM	Stanton
56092	E	E	WNXX	DD	
56093	F	E	WNXX	DD	
56094	E	E	WGAT	TE	Eggborough Power Station
56095	E	E	WGAT	TE	
56096	E	E	WGAI	IM	
56098	F	E	WGAT	TE	

56099	F	E	WGAI	IM	
56100	LH	E	WGAI	IM	
56101	F	E	WNXX	IM	Mutual Improvement
56102	LH	E	WGAI	IM	
56103	E	E	WGAI	IM	STORA
56104	F	E	WNXX	IM	
56105	E	E	WGAT	TE	
56106	LH	E	WGAT	TE	
56107	LH	E	WGAI	IM	
56108	F	E	WNXX	TE	
56109	LH	E	WGAT	TE	
56110	LH	E	WGAI	IM	Croft[1]
56111	LH	E	WGAI	IM	
56112	LH	E	WGAI	IM	Stainless Pioneer
56113	E	E	WGAI	IM	
56114	E	E	WGAT	TE	
56115	E	E	WGAI	IM	Bassetlaw
56116	LH	E	WGAI	IM	
56117	E	E	WGAT	TE	
56118	LH	E	WGAI	IM	
56119	E	E	WGAT	TE	
56120	E	E	WGAI	IM	
56121	F	E	WNYX	kd	
56123	F	E	WNYX	IM	Drax Power Station
56124	F	E	WNYX	KY	
56125	F	E	WNXX	IM	
56127	F	E	WGAT	TE	
56128	F	E	WNXX	IM	
56129	F	E	WGAI	IM	
56130	LH	E	WNXX	TT	Wardley Opencast
56131	F	E	WGAI	IM	Ellington Colliery
56132	F	E	WNYX	TT	
56133	F	E	WNXX	TO	
56134	F	E	WGAT	TE	Blyth Power
56135	F	E	WNYX	IM	Port of Tyne Authority

CLASS 57   BRUSH/GM   Co-Co

Built: 1964–65 by Brush Traction at Loughborough or BR at Crewe Works as Class 47. Rebuilt 1997–2000 by Brush Traction at Loughborough.
Engine: General Motors 645-12E3 of 1860 kW (2500 h.p.) at 900 r.p.m.
Main Alternator: Brush BA1101A.
Traction Motors: Brush TM68-46.
Maximum Tractive Effort: 244.5 kN (55000 lbf).
Continuous Tractive Effort: 140 kN (31500 lbf) at ?? m.p.h.
Power at Rail: 1507 kW (2025 h.p.).   **Train Brakes:** Air.
Brake Force: 80 t.   **Dimensions:** 19.38 x 2.79 m.
Weight: 120.6 t.   **Wheel Diameter:** 1143 mm.
Design Speed: 75 m.p.h.   **Maximum Speed:** 75 m.p.h.
Fuel Capacity: 3273 (+ 5550 litres).   **RA:** 6
Train Supply: Not equipped.   **Multiple Working:** Not equipped.

57001	(47356)	**FL**	P	DFHZ	CD	Freightliner Pioneer
57002	(47322)	**FL**	P	DFHZ	CD	Freightliner Phoenix
57003	(47317)	**FL**	P	DFHZ	CD	Freightliner Evolution
57004	(47347)	**FL**	P	DFHZ	CD	Freightliner Quality
57005	(47350)	**FL**	P	DFHZ	CD	Freightliner Excellence
57006	(47187)	**FL**	P	DFHZ	CD	Freightliner Reliance
57007	(47332)	**FL**	P	DFHZ	CD	Freightliner Bond
57008	(47060)	**FL**	P	DFHZ	CD	Freightliner Explorer
57009	(47079)	**FL**	P	DFHZ	CD	Freightliner Venturer
57010	(47231)	**FL**	P	DFHZ	CD	Freightliner Crusader
57011	(47329)	**FL**	P	DFHZ	CD	Freightliner Challenger
57012	(47204)	+ **FL**	P	DFTZ	CD	Freightliner Envoy

Class 57/6. Electric Train Supply Equipment. Details as Class 57/0 except:
Fuel Capacity: 5887 litres. **Train Supply:** Electric, index 95.

57601	(47825)	**P**	P	IWLA	LE	Thomas Telford

CLASS 58   BREL/PAXMAN   Co-Co

Built: 1983–87 by BREL at Doncaster Works.
Engine: Ruston Paxman 12RK3ACT of 2460 kW (3300 h.p.) at 1000 r.p.m.
Main Alternator: Brush BA1101B.   **Traction Motors:** Brush TM73-62.
Maximum Tractive Effort: 275 kN (61800 lbf).
Continuous Tractive Effort: 240 kN (53950 lbf) at 17.4 m.p.h.
Power At Rail: 1780 kW (2387 h.p.).   **Train Brakes:** Air.
Brake Force: 62 t.   **Dimensions:** 19.13 x 2.72 m.
Weight: 130 t.   **Wheel Diameter:** 1120 mm.
Design Speed: 80 m.p.h.   **Maximum Speed:** 80 m.p.h.
Fuel Capacity: 4214 litres.   **RA:** 7.
Train Supply: Not equipped.   **Multiple Working:** Red Diamond.

Note: All equipped with Slow Speed Control.

58001	**F**	E	WNXX	KY	
58002	**ML**	E	WNXX	EH	Daw Mill Colliery
58003	**F**	E	WNXX	TO	Markham Colliery
58004	**F**	E	WNXX	DD	
58005	**ML**	E	WNXX	LR	Ironbridge Power Station
58006	**F**	E	WNXX	IW	
58007	**F**	E	WNXX	IW	
58008	**ML**	E	WNXX	TO	
58009	**F**	E	WFAH	EH	
58010	**F**	E	WNXX	IP	
58011	**F**	E	WNXX	IP	
58012	**F**	E	WNXX	DD	
58013	**ML**	E	WNXX	EH	
58014	**ML**	E	WNXX	TO	
58015	**F**	E	WNXX	DD	
58016	**E**	E	WFAH	EH	
58017	**F**	E	WNXX	DD	
58018	**F**	E	WNXX	IP	High Marnham Power Station

58019	F	E	WNXX	TO	Shirebrook Colliery
58020	F	E	WFAH	EH	Doncaster Works
58021	ML	E	WFAH	EH	Hither Green Depot
58022	F	E	WNXX	CD	
58023	ML	E	WNXX	TO	
58024	E	E	WFAH	EH	
58025	F	E	WFAH	EH	
58026	F	E	WFAH	EH	
58027	F	E	WNXX	DD	
58028	F	E	WNXX	TO	
58029	F	E	WFAH	EH	
58030	E	E	WFAH	EH	
58031	F	E	WFAH	EH	
58032	ML	E	WNXX	IP	Thoresby Colliery
58033	E	E	WFAH	EH	
58034	F	E	WNXX	DD	
58035	F	E	WNXX	DD	
58036	ML	E	WFGA	DR	
58037	E	E	WFAH	EH	Worksop Depot
58038	ML	E	WFGA	TO	
58039	E	E	WFGA	TO	
58040	F	E	WNXX	IP	Cottam Power Station
58041	F	E	WFAH	EH	Ratcliffe Power Station
58042	ML	E	WFAH	EH	
58043	F	E	WFAH	EH	
58044	F	E	WFGA	CD	
58045	F	E	WFAH	EH	
58046	ML	E	WFGA	DR	Asfordby Mine
58047	E	E	WFAH	EH	
58048	E	E	WNXX	TO	
58049	E	E	WFAH	EH	Littleton Colliery
58050	E	E	WFAH	EH	Toton Traction Depot

CLASS 59   GENERAL MOTORS   Co-Co

Built: 1985 (59001/002/004) or 1989 (59005) by General Motors, La Grange, Illinois, USA or 1990 (59101–4), 1994 (59201) and 1995 (59202–6) by General Motors, London, Ontario, Canada.
Engine: General Motors 645E3C two stroke of 2460 kW (3300 h.p.) at 900 r.p.m.
Main Alternator: General Motors AR11 MLD-D14A.
Traction Motors: General Motors D77B.
Maximum Tractive Effort: 506 kN (113 550 lbf).
Continuous Tractive Effort: 291 kN (65 300 lbf) at 14.3 m.p.h.
Power At Rail: 1889 kW (2533 h.p.).   **Train Brakes:** Air.
Brake Force: 69 t.   **Dimensions:** 21.35 x 2.65 m.
Weight: 121 t.   **Wheel Diameter:** 1067 mm.
Design Speed: 60 (* 75) m.p.h.   **Maximum Speed:** 60 (* 75) m.p.h.
Fuel Capacity: 4546 litres.   **RA:** 7.
Train Supply: Not equipped.   **Multiple Working:** AAR System.

Class 59/0. Owned by Foster-Yeoman.

59001	**FY**	FY	XYPO	MD	YEOMAN ENDEAVOUR
59002	**MR**	FY	XYPO	MD	ALAN J DAY
59004	**YO**	FY	XYPO	MD	PAUL A HAMMOND
59005	**FY**	FY	XYPO	MD	KENNETH J PAINTER

Class 59/1. Owned by Hanson Quarry Products.

59101	**HA**	HA	XYPA	MD	Village of Whatley
59102	**HA**	HA	XYPA	MD	Village of Chantry
59103	**HA**	HA	XYPA	MD	Village of Mells
59104	**HA**	HA	XYPA	MD	Village of Great Elm

Class 59/2. Owned by English Welsh & Scottish Railway.

59201 *	**E**	E	WDAG	HG	Vale of York
59202 *	**E**	E	WDAG	HG	Vale of White Horse
59203 *	**E**	E	WDAG	HG	Vale of Pickering
59204 *	**E**	E	WDAG	HG	Vale of Glamorgan
59205 b*	**E**	E	WDAG	HG	L. Keith McNair
59206 b*	**E**	E	WDAG	HG	Pride of Ferrybridge

CLASS 60   BRUSH/MIRRLEES   Co-Co

Built: 1989–1993 by Brush Traction at Loughborough.
Engine: Mirrlees 8MB275T of 2310 kW (3100 h.p.) at 1000 r.p.m.
Main Alternator: Brush BA1000.   **Traction Motors:** Brush TM216.
Maximum Tractive Effort: 500 kN (106500 lbf).
Continuous Tractive Effort: 336 kN (71570 lbf) at 17.4 m.p.h.
Power At Rail: 1800 kW (2415 h.p.).   **Train Brakes:** Air.
Brake Force: 74 (+ 62) t.   **Dimensions:** 21.34 x 2.64 m.
Weight: 129 (+ 131) t.   **Wheel Diameter:** 1118 mm.
Design Speed: 62 m.p.h.   **Maximum Speed:** 60 m.p.h.
Fuel Capacity: 4546 (+ 5225) litres.   **RA:** 7.
Train Supply: Not equipped.   **Multiple Working:** Within class.

Note: All equipped with Slow Speed Control.

Non-standard livery: 60006/033 are in "Corus" livery of silver with red logos.

60001		**E**	E	WCAT	TE	The Railway Observer
60002	+	**E**	E	WCAT	TE	
60003	+	**E**	E	WCAK	CF	FREIGHT TRANSPORT ASSOCIATION
60004	+	**E**	E	WCAK	CF	
60005	+	**E**	E	WCAK	CF	BP Gas Avonmouth
60006		**O**	E	WCAT	TE	Scunthorpe Ironmaster
60007		**LH**	E	WCAI	IM	
60008		**LH**	E	WCAT	TE	GYPSUM QUEEN II
60009	+	**F**	E	WCAI	IM	Carnedd Dafydd
60010	+	**E**	E	WCAK	CF	
60011		**ML**	E	WCAT	TE	
60012	+	**E**	E	WCAI	IM	
60013		**F**	E	WCAT	TE	Robert Boyle
60014		**F**	E	WCAT	TE	Alexander Fleming

60015 +	F	E	WCAK	CF	Bow Fell
60016	E	E	WCAN	TO	RAIL Magazine
60017 +	E	E	WCAT	TE	Shotton Works Centenary Year 1996
60018	E	E	WCAT	TE	
60019	E	E	WCAN	TO	
60020 +	E	E	WCAI	IM	
60021 +	F	E	WCAI	IM	Pen-y-Ghent[1]
60022 +	E	E	WCAI	IM	
60023 +	E	E	WCAI	IM	
60024 +	E	E	WCAN	TO	
60025 +	E	E	WCAI	IM	Caledonian Paper
60026 +	E	E	WCAK	CF	
60027 +	E	E	WCAI	IM	
60028 +	F	E	WCAI	IM	John Flamsteed
60029	E	E	WCAN	TO	Clitheroe Castle
60030 +	E	E	WCAK	CF	
60031	F	E	WCAN	TO	
60032	F	E	WCAN	TO	William Booth
60033 +	O	E	WCAT	TE	Tees Steel Express
60034	F	E	WCAN	TO	Carnedd Llewelyn[1]
60035	F	E	WCAT	TE	
60036	E	E	WCAN	TO	GEFCO
60037 +	E	E	WCAK	CF	Aberthaw/Aberddawan
60038 +	LH	E	WCAI	IM	
60039	E	E	WCAT	TE	
60040	E	E	WCAT	TE	
60041 +	E	E	WCAK	CF	
60042 +	E	E	WCAT	TE	The Hundred of Hoo
60043	E	E	WCAT	TE	
60044	ML	E	WCAT	TE	
60045	E	E	WCAT	TE	The Permanent Way Institution
60046 +	F	E	WCAN	TO	William Wilberforce[1]
60047 +	E	E	WCAN	TO	
60048	E	E	WCAT	TE	EASTERN
60049 +	E	E	WCAT	TE	
60050 +	E	E	WCAT	TE	
60051 +	E	E	WCAK	CF	
60052 +	E	E	WCAK	CF	Glofa Twr – The last deep mine in
60053 +	E	E	WCAT	TE	NORDIC TERMINAL
60054 +	F	E	WCAN	TO	Charles Babbage
60055 +	F	E	WCAI	IM	Thomas Barnardo
60056 +	F	E	WCAK	CF	William Beveridge
60057	F	E	WCAN	TO	Adam Smith
60058 +	F	E	WCAI	IM	John Howard
60059 +	LH	E	WCAK	CF	Swinden Dalesman
60060	F	E	WCAT	TE	James Watt
60061	F	E	WCAT	TE	Alexander Graham Bell
60062	F	E	WCAT	TE	Samuel Johnson
60063	F	E	WCAT	TE	James Murray
60064 +	F	E	WCAK	CF	Back Tor[1]
60065	F	E	WCAT	TE	Kinder Low[1]

60066	F	E	WCAN	TO	John Logie Baird
60067 +	F	E	WCAN	TO	James Clerk-Maxwell
60068	F	E	WCAN	TO	Charles Darwin
60069	F	E	WCAN	TO	Humphry Davy
60070 +	F	E	WCAK	CF	John Loudon McAdam
60071 +	F	E	WCAN	TO	Dorothy Garrod
60072	F	E	WCAN	TO	Cairn Toul[1]
60073	F	E	WCAT	TE	Cairn Gorm[1]
60074	F	E	WCAT	TE	
60075	F	E	WCAN	TO	
60076	F	E	WCAN	TO	
60077 +	F	E	WCAK	CF	Canisp[1]
60078	ML	E	WCAT	TE	
60079	F	E	WCAT	TE	Foinaven
60080 +	E	E	WCAI	IM	Cloudside Junior School
60081 +	GW	E	WCAK	CF	ISAMBARD KINGDOM BRUNEL
60082	F	E	WCAT	TE	Mam Tor
60083	E	E	WCAT	TE	Mountsorrel
60084	F	E	WCAN	TO	Cross Fell
60085	F	E	WCAT	TE	MINI Spirit of Oxford
60086	F	E	WCAT	TE	Schiehallion
60087	F	E	WCAN	TO	Slioch
60088	F	E	WCAT	TE	Buachaille Etive Mor[1]
60089 +	F	E	WCAK	CF	Arcuil
60090 +	F	E	WCAI	IM	Quinag
60091 +	F	E	WCAK	CF	An Teallach
60092	F	E	WCAT	TE	Reginald Munns
60093	F	E	WCAT	TE	Jack Stirk
60094	F	E	WCAN	TO	Tryfan
60095	F	E	WCAN	TO	
60096 +	F	E	WCAK	CF	Ben Macdui
60097 +	F	E	WCAI	IM	
60098 +	E	E	WCAK	CF	Charles Francis Brush
60099	F	E	WCAT	TE	Ben More Assynt
60100	F	E	WCAN	TO	Boar of Badenoch

CLASS 66   GENERAL MOTORS   Co-Co

Built: 1998–2001 by General Motors, London, Ontario, Canada (Model JT42CWR).
Engine: General Motors 12N-710G3B-EC two stroke of 2385 kW (3200 h.p.) at 900 r.p.m.
Main Alternator: General Motors AR8/C86.
Traction Motors: General Motors D43TR.
Maximum Tractive Effort: 409 kN (92000 lbf).
Continuous Tractive Effort: 260 kN (58390 lbf) at 15.9 m.p.h.
Power At Rail: 1850 kW (2480 h.p.).   **Train Brakes:** Air.
Brake Force: 68 t.   **Dimensions:** 21.35 x 2.64 m.
Weight: 126 t.   **Wheel Diameter:** 1120 mm.
Design Speed: 87.5 m.p.h.   **Maximum Speed:** 75 m.p.h.
Fuel Capacity: 6550 litres.   **RA:** 7.
Train Supply: Not equipped.   **Multiple Working:** AAR System.

Notes:

All equipped with Slow Speed Control.
k Fitted with Slow Speed Control and Swinghead Automatic Combination Couplers.
Locos in pool WBBM are fitted with RETB.

Class 66/0. EWS operated locomotives.

66001		E	A	WBAT	TE	66044		E	A	WBAT	TE
66002		E	A	WBAN	TO	66045	k	E	A	WBAI	IM
66003	k	E	A	WBAT	TE	66046	k	E	A	WBAI	IM
66004		E	A	WBAN	TO	66047	k	E	A	WBAT	TE
66005	k	E	A	WBAI	IM	66048		E	A	WBAI	IM
66006		E	A	WBAT	TE	66049		E	A	WBAM	ML
66007		E	A	WBAI	IM	66050		E	A	WBAI	IM
66008	k	E	A	WBAK	CF	66051	k	E	A	WBAT	TE
66009	k	E	A	WBAH	EH	66052		E	A	WBAI	IM
66010		E	A	WBAI	IM	66053		E	A	WBAI	IM
66011	k	E	A	WBAI	IM	66054	k	E	A	WBAK	CF
66012		E	A	WBAI	IM	66055		E	A	WBAK	CF
66013		E	A	WBAH	EH	66056		E	A	WBAK	CF
66014	k	E	A	WBAI	IM	66057		E	A	WBAK	CF
66015		E	A	WBAH	EH	66058		E	A	WBAK	CF
66016	k	E	A	WBAH	EH	66059		E	A	WBAN	TO
66017		E	A	WBAN	TO	66060		E	A	WBAI	IM
66018		E	A	WBAI	IM	66061		E	A	WBAH	EH
66019	k	E	A	WBAK	CF	66062		E	A	WBAN	TO
66020	k	E	A	WBAT	TE	66063		E	A	WBAI	IM
66021		E	A	WBAK	CF	66064		E	A	WBAH	EH
66022		E	A	WBAN	TO	66065		E	A	WBAM	ML
66023		E	A	WBAI	IM	66066		E	A	WBAM	ML
66024		E	A	WBAN	TO	66067		E	A	WBAN	TO
66025		E	A	WBAN	TO	66068		E	A	WBAI	IM
66026	k	E	A	WBAI	IM	66069		E	A	WBAI	IM
66027	k	E	A	WBAI	IM	66070		E	A	WBAT	TE
66028		E	A	WBAM	ML	66071		E	A	WBAI	IM
66029	k	E	A	WBAK	CF	66072		E	A	WBAI	IM
66030		E	A	WBAT	TE	66073		E	A	WBAI	IM
66031	k	E	A	WBAK	CF	66074		E	A	WBAN	TO
66032	k	E	A	WBAK	CF	66075		E	A	WBAN	TO
66033		E	A	WBAH	EH	66076		E	A	WBAK	CF
66034		E	A	WBAH	EH	66077	k	E	A	WBAI	IM
66035		E	A	WBAM	ML	66078		E	A	WBAT	TE
66036	k	E	A	WBAI	IM	66079		E	A	WBAK	CF
66037	k	E	A	WBAN	TO	66080	k	E	A	WBAK	CF
66038		E	A	WBAN	TO	66081		E	A	WBAI	IM
66039	k	E	A	WBAI	IM	66082		E	A	WBAH	EH
66040		E	A	WBAN	TO	66083		E	A	WBAT	TE
66041	k	E	A	WBAT	TE	66084	k	E	A	WBAI	IM
66042		E	A	WBAN	TO	66085		E	A	WBAI	IM
66043	k	E	A	WBAK	CF	66086		E	A	WBAN	TO

66087		E	A	WBAN	TO	66138	E	A	WBAT	TE
66088		E	A	WBAK	CF	66139	E	A	WBAI	IM
66089		E	A	WBAT	TE	66140	E	A	WBAT	TE
66090		E	A	WBAK	CF	66141	E	A	WBAI	IM
66091		E	A	WBAI	IM	66142	E	A	WBAN	TO
66092		E	A	WBAK	CF	66143	E	A	WBAK	CF
66093	k	E	A	WBAT	TE	66144	E	A	WBAK	CF
66094	k	E	A	WBAI	IM	66145	E	A	WBAK	CF
66095	k	E	A	WBBM	ML	66146	E	A	WBAH	EH
66096		E	A	WBBM	ML	66147	E	A	WBAI	IM
66097		E	A	WBAM	ML	66148	E	A	WBAN	TO
66098		E	A	WBBM	ML	66149	E	A	WBAT	TE
66099		E	A	WBBM	ML	66150	E	A	WBAN	TO
66100		E	A	WBBM	ML	66151	E	A	WBAK	CF
66101		E	A	WBAM	ML	66152	E	A	WBAM	ML
66102	k	E	A	WBBM	ML	66153	E	A	WBAI	IM
66103		E	A	WBBM	ML	66154	E	A	WBAI	IM
66104		E	A	WBBM	ML	66155	E	A	WBAI	IM
66105		E	A	WBBM	ML	66156	k	E	A	WBAT	TE
66106		E	A	WBBM	ML	66157	E	A	WBAK	CF
66107		E	A	WBAM	ML	66158	k	E	A	WBAI	IM
66108		E	A	WBBM	ML	66159	E	A	WBAN	TO
66109	k	E	A	WBBM	ML	66160	E	A	WBAI	IM
66110		E	A	WBBM	ML	66161	E	A	WBAT	TE
66111		E	A	WBBM	ML	66162	E	A	WBAH	EH
66112		E	A	WBBM	ML	66163	k	E	A	WBAN	TO
66113		E	A	WBBM	ML	66164	k	E	A	WBAK	CF
66114	k	E	A	WBAM	ML	66165	k	E	A	WBAK	CF
66115		E	A	WBAK	CF	66166	E	A	WBAI	IM
66116		E	A	WBAM	ML	66167	E	A	WBAI	IM
66117		E	A	WBAN	TO	66168	E	A	WBAK	CF
66118		E	A	WBAT	TE	66169	E	A	WBAH	EH
66119		E	A	WBAN	TO	66170	k	E	A	WBAT	TE
66120	k	E	A	WBAI	IM	66171	k	E	A	WBAN	TO
66121		E	A	WBAI	IM	66172	E	A	WBAI	IM
66122		E	A	WBAH	EH	66173	E	A	WBAH	EH
66123		E	A	WBAI	IM	66174	E	A	WBAN	TO
66124		E	A	WBAI	IM	66175	E	A	WBAN	TO
66125	k	E	A	WBAT	TE	66176	E	A	WBAK	CF
66126		E	A	WBAN	TO	66177	k	E	A	WBAI	IM
66127		E	A	WBAK	CF	66178	E	A	WBAN	TO
66128		E	A	WBAI	IM	66179	E	A	WBAK	CF
66129		E	A	WBAN	TO	66180	E	A	WBAM	ML
66130	k	E	A	WBAI	IM	66181	E	A	WBAK	CF
66131		E	A	WBAI	IM	66182	k	E	A	WBAN	TO
66132		E	A	WBAH	EH	66183	k	E	A	WBAI	IM
66133		E	A	WBAM	ML	66184	E	A	WBAT	TE
66134		E	A	WBAI	IM	66185	E	A	WBAI	IM
66135		E	A	WBAK	CF	66186	E	A	WBAM	ML
66136		E	A	WBAM	ML	66187	E	A	WBAK	CF
66137		E	A	WBAI	IM	66188	E	A	WBAN	TO

66189		E	A	WBAH	EH	66220	k	E	A	WBAI	IM
66190		E	A	WBAT	TE	66221	k	E	A	WBAI	IM
66191		E	A	WBAK	CF	66222	k	E	A	WBAK	CF
66192	k	E	A	WBAT	TE	66223	k	E	A	WBAT	TE
66193		E	A	WBAM	ML	66224	k	E	A	WBAT	TE
66194		E	A	WBAN	TO	66225	k	E	A	WBAN	TO
66195	k	E	A	WBAN	TO	66226	k	E	A	WBAI	IM
66196		E	A	WBAN	TO	66227	k	E	A	WBAT	TE
66197		E	A	WBAI	IM	66228	k	E	A	WBAI	IM
66198		E	A	WBAT	TE	66229	k	E	A	WBAK	CF
66199		E	A	WBAK	CF	66230	k	E	A	WBAI	IM
66200		E	A	WBAM	ML	66231	k	E	A	WBAN	TO
66201	k	E	A	WBAI	IM	66232	k	E	A	WBAN	TO
66202	k	E	A	WBAK	CF	66233	k	E	A	WBAT	TE
66203	k	E	A	WBAT	TE	66234	k	E	A	WBAI	IM
66204	k	E	A	WBAI	IM	66235	k	E	A	WBAK	CF
66205	k	E	A	WBAI	IM	66236	k	E	A	WBAK	CF
66206	k	E	A	WBAK	CF	66237	k	E	A	WBAI	IM
66207	k	E	A	WBAI	IM	66238	k	E	A	WBAH	EH
66208	k	E	A	WBAN	TO	66239	k	E	A	WBAK	CF
66209	k	E	A	WBAI	IM	66240	k	E	A	WBAI	IM
66210	k	E	A	WBAN	TO	66241	k	E	A	WBAK	CF
66211	k	E	A	WBAT	TE	66242	k	E	A	WBAI	IM
66212	k	E	A	WBAK	CF	66243	k	E	A	WBAN	TO
66213	k	E	A	WBAI	IM	66244	k	E	A	WBAT	TE
66214	k	E	A	WBAK	CF	66245	k	E	A	WBAI	IM
66215	k	E	A	WBAK	CF	66246	k	E	A	WBAN	TO
66216	k	E	A	WBAH	EH	66247	k	E	A	WBAN	TO
66217	k	E	A	WBAH	EH	66248	k	E	A	WBAM	ML
66218	k	E	A	WBAN	TO	66249	k	E	A	WBAH	EH
66219	k	E	A	WBAN	TO	66250	k	E	A	WBAK	CF

Class 66/5. Freightliner operated locomotives.
Details as Class 66/0.

66501	FL	P	DFGM	CD	Japan 2001
66502	FL	P	DFGM	CD	Basford Hall Centenary 2001
66503	FL	P	DFGM	CD	
66504	FL	P	DFGM	CD	
66505	FL	P	DFGM	CD	
66506	FL	H	DFRT	CD	Crewe Regeneration
66507	FL	H	DFRT	CD	
66508	FL	H	DFRT	CD	
66509	FL	H	DFRT	CD	
66510	FL	H	DFRT	CD	
66511	FL	H	DFRT	CD	
66512	FL	H	DFRT	CD	
66513	FL	H	DFRT	CD	
66514	FL	H	DFRT	CD	
66515	FL	H	DFRT	CD	
66516	FL	H	DFRT	CD	
66517	FL	H	DFRT	CD	

66518	**FL**	H	DFRT	CD	
66519	**FL**	H	DFRT	CD	
66520	**FL**	H	DFRT	CD	
66521	**FL**	H	DHLT	ZF	
66522	**FL**	H	DFHH	CD	
66523	**FL**	H	DFHH	CD	
66524	**FL**	H	DFHH	CD	
66525	**FL**	H	DFHH	CD	
66526	**FL**	P	DFHH	CD	Steve Dunn
66527	**FL**	P	DFHH	CD	Don Raider
66528	**FL**	P	DFHH	CD	
66529	**FL**	P	DFHH	CD	
66530	**FL**	P	DFHH	CD	
66531	**FL**	P	DFHH	CD	
66532	**FL**	P	DFGM	CD	
66533	**FL**	P	DFGM	CD	
66534	**FL**	P	DFGM	CD	OOCL Express
66535	**FL**	P	DFGM	CD	
66536	**FL**	P	DFGM	CD	
66537	**FL**	P	DFGM	CD	
66538	**FL**	H	DFGM	CD	
66539	**FL**	H	DFGM	CD	
66540	**FL**	H	DFGM	CD	
66541	**FL**	H	DFGM	CD	
66542	**FL**	H	DFGM		
66543	**FL**	H	DFGM		
66544	**FL**	P	DFHH		
66545	**FL**	P	DFHH		
66546	**FL**	P	DFHH		
66547	**FL**	P	DFHH		
66548	**FL**	P	DFHH		
66549	**FL**	P	DFHH		
66550	**FL**	P	DFHH		
66551	**FL**	P	DFHH		
66552	**FL**	P	DFHH		
66553	**FL**	P	DFHH		
66554	**FL**	H	DFHH		

Class 66/6. Freightliner operated locomotives with modified gear ratios.
Details as Class 66/0 except:
Maximum Tractive Effort: 467 kN (105080 lbf).
Continuous Tractive Effort: 296 kN (66630 lbf) at 14.0 m.p.h.
Design Speed: 87.5 m.p.h.　　　　**Maximum Speed:** 65 m.p.h.

66601	**FL**	P	DFHH	CD	The Hope Valley
66602	**FL**	P	DFRT	CD	
66603	**FL**	P	DFRT	CD	
66604	**FL**	P	DFRT	CD	
66605	**FL**	P	DFRT	CD	
66606	**FL**	P	DFRT	CD	
66607	**FL**	P	DFHH		
66608	**FL**	P	DFHH		

66609	FL	P	DFHH
66610	FL	P	DFHH
66611	FL	P	DFHH
66612	FL	P	DFHH

Class 66/7. GB Railfreight operated locomotives. Details as Class 66/0.

66701	GB	H	GBZZ	WN	Railtrack National Logistics
66702	GB	H	GBZZ	WN	
66703	GB	H	GBZZ	WN	
66704	GB	H	GBZZ	WN	
66705	GB	H	GBZZ	WN	
66706	GB	H	GBZZ	WN	
66707	GB	H	GBZZ	WN	
66708	GB				
66709	GB				
66710	GB				
66711	GB				
66712	GB				

CLASS 67   GENERAL MOTORS   Bo-Bo

Built: 1999–2000 by Alstom at Valencia, Spain, as sub-contractors for General Motors (General Motors model JT42 HW-HS).
Engine: General Motors 12N-710G3B-EC two stroke of 2385 kW (3200 h.p.) at 900 r.p.m.
Main Alternator: General Motors AR9/HE3/CA6B.
Traction Motors: General Motors D43FM.
Maximum Tractive Effort: 141 kN (31750 lbf).
Continuous Tractive Effort: 90 kN (20200 lbf) at ?? m.p.h.
Power At Rail: 1860 kW.   **Train Brakes:** Air.
Brake Force: 78 t.   **Dimensions:** 19.74 x 2.72 m.
Weight: 90 t.   **Wheel Diameter:** 965 mm.
Design Speed: 125 m.p.h.   **Maximum Speed:** 110 (*125) m.p.h.
Fuel Capacity: 4927 litres.   **RA:** 8.
Train Supply: Electric, index 66.   **Multiple Working:** AAR System.
Note: All equipped with Slow Speed Control and Swinghead Automatic Combination Couplers.

67001	E	A	WAAK	CF	Night Mail
67002	E	A	WNWX	ZF	Special Delivery
67003	E	A	WAAK	CF	
67004	E	A	WAAK	CF	Poste Haste
67005	E	A	WAAK	CF	Queen's Messenger
67006	E	A	WAAK	CF	
67007	E	A	WAAK	CF	
67008	E	A	WAAK	CF	
67009	E	A	WAAK	CF	
67010	E	A	WAAK	CF	Unicorn
67011	E	A	WAAK	CF	
67012	E	A	WAAK	CF	
67013	E	A	WAAK	CF	

67014		E	A	WAAK	CF	
67015		E	A	WAAK	CF	
67016		E	A	WAAK	CF	
67017		E	A	WAAK	CF	
67018		E	A	WAAK	CF	
67019		E	A	WAAK	CF	
67020		E	A	WAAK	CF	
67021		E	A	WAAK	CF	
67022		E	A	WAAK	CF	
67023	*	E	A	WAAK	CF	
67024		E	A	WAAK	CF	
67025		E	A	WAAK	CF	Western Star
67026		E	A	WAAK	CF	
67027		E	A	WAAK	CF	
67028		E	A	WAAK	CF	
67029		E	A	WAAK	CF	
67030		E	A	WAAK	CF	

2. ELECTRIC & ELECTRO-DIESEL LOCOMOTIVES

CLASS 73/0   BR/ENGLISH ELECTRIC   Bo-Bo

Electro-diesel locomotives which can operate either from a d.c supply or using power from a diesel engine.

Built: 1962 by BR at Eastleigh Works.
Engine: English Electric 4SRKT of 447 kW (600 h.p.) at 850 r.p.m.
Main Generator: English Electric 824/3D.
Electric Supply System: 750 V d.c. from third rail.
Traction Motors: English Electric 542A.
Maximum Tractive Effort (Electric): Electric 187 kN (42000 lbf).
Maximum Tractive Effort (Diesel): 152 kN (34100 lbf).
Continuous Rating (Electric): 1060 kW (1420 h.p.) giving a tractive effort of 43 kN (9600 lbf) at 55.5 m.p.h.
Continuous Tractive Effort (Diesel): 72 kN (16100 lbf) at 10 m.p.h.
Maximum Rail Power (Electric): 1830 kW (2450 h.p.) at 37 m.p.h.
Train Brakes: Air, vacuum & electro-pneumatic († Air & electro-pneumatic).
Brake Force: 31 t.   **Dimensions:** 16.36 x 2.64 m.
Weight: 76.3 t.   **Wheel Diameter:** 1016 mm.
Design Speed: 80 m.p.h.   **Maximum Speed:** 60 m.p.h.
Fuel Capacity: 1545 litres.   **RA:** 6.
Train Supply: Electric, index 66 (on electric power only). May also deliver a reduced electric train supply when on diesel power whilst stationary.
Multiple Working: SR System.
Non-standard livery: 73005 is in non-standard blue livery with white roof.

Formerly numbered E 6001–6.

Note: Locomotives numbered in the 739XX series are classed as 73/9 and were renumbered when they were transferred to Merseyrail. All four remaining locos are in departmental service and are used for de-icing and sandite duties.

73901	†	**MS**	ME	HEBD	BD	73005	**0**	ME HEBD	BD
73002		**BL**	ME	HEBD	BD	73906	† **MS**	ME HEBD	BD

CLASS 73/1   BR/ENGLISH ELECTRIC   Bo-Bo

Electro-diesel locomotives which can operate either from a d.c supply or using power from a diesel engine.

Built: 1965–67 by English Electric Co. at Vulcan Foundry, Newton le Willows.
Main Generator: English Electric 824/5D.
Traction Motors: English Electric 546/1B.
Maximum Tractive Effort (Electric): 179 kN (40000 lbf).

Maximum Tractive Effort (Diesel): 160 kN (36000 lbf).
Continuous Rating (Electric): 1060 kW (1420 h.p.) giving a tractive effort of 35 kN (7800 lbf) at 68 m.p.h.
Continuous Tractive Effort (Diesel): 60 kN (13600 lbf) at 11.5 m.p.h.
Maximum Rail Power (Electric): 2350 kW (3150 h.p.) at 42 m.p.h.
Train Brakes: Air, vacuum & electro-pneumatic († Air & electro-pneumatic).
Brake Force: 31 t.   **Dimensions:** 16.36 x 2.64 m.
Weight: 77 t.   **Wheel Diameter:** 1016 mm.
Design Speed: 90 m.p.h.   **Maximum Speed:** 90 m.p.h.
Fuel Capacity: 1409 litres.
Train Supply: Electric, index 66 (on electric power only).
Multiple Working: SR System.

Formerly numbered E 6001–20/22–26/28–49 (not in order).

Note: Locomotives numbered in the 732XX series are classed as 73/2 and were originally dedicated to Gatwick Express services.

73101	PC	E	WPAG	HG	The Royal Alex'
73103	IM	E	WNXX	EH	
73104	IM	E	WNZX	EH	
73105	CE	E	WNZX	OM	
73106	DG	E	WNXX	HG	
73107	CE	E	WNXX	OM	Redhill 1844–1994
73108	CE	E	WPAG	HG	
73109	ST	SW	HYSB	BM	Battle of Britain 50th Anniversary
73110	CE	E	WPAG	HG	
73114	ML	E	WNZX	OM	
73117	IM	E	WNXX	EH	University of Surrey
73118 †c	EP	EU	GPSN	OC	
73128	CE	E	WNXX	OM	Kentish Mercury
73129	N	E	WPAG	HG	City of Winchester
73130 †c	EP	EU	GPSN	OC	
73131	E	E	WPAG	HG	
73132	IM	E	WNZX	OM	
73133	ML	E	WPAG	HG	The Bluebell Railway
73134	IM	E	WNXX	EH	Woking Homes 1885–1985
73136	ML	E	WPAG	HG	Kent Youth Music
73138	CE	E	WNXX	OM	
73139	IM	E	WNZX	EH	
73140	IM	E	WNZX	OM	
73141	IM	E	WNZX	OM	
73201 †	GX	P	IVGA	SL	
73202 †	GX	P	IVGA	SL	
73203 †	GX	P	GBZZ	SL (S)	
73204 †	GX	P	GBZZ	SU (S)	
73205 †	GX	P	GBZZ	SL (S)	
73206 †	GX	P	GBZZ	PY (S)	
73207 †	GX	P	GBZZ	PY (S)	
73208 †	GX	P	IVGA	SL	
73209 †	GX	P	GBZZ	PY (S)	

73210	†	**GX**	P	IVGA	SL
73211	†	**GX**	P	IVGA	SL
73212	†	**GX**	RK	QAED	DF
73213	†	**GX**	P	GBZZ	PY (S)
73235	†	**GX**	P	IVGA	SL

CLASS 86   BR/ENGLISH   ELECTRIC   Bo-Bo

Built: 1965–66 by English Electric Co. at Vulcan Foundry, Newton le Willows or by BR at Doncaster Works.
Electric Supply System: 25 kV a.c. 50 Hz overhead.
Traction Motors: AEI 282BZ axle hung.
Maximum Tractive Effort: 207 kN (46500 lbf).
Continuous Rating: 3010 kW (4040 h.p.) giving a tractive effort of 85 kN (19200 lbf) at 77.5 m.p.h.
Maximum Rail Power: 4550 kW (6100 h.p.) at 49.5 m.p.h.

Train Brakes: Air.	**Brake Force:** 40 t.
Dimensions: 17.83 x 2.65 m.	**Weight:** 83–86.8 t.
Wheel Diameter: 1156 mm.	**Design Speed:** 100 m.p.h.
Maximum Speed: 100 m.p.h.	**Train Supply:** Electric, index 74.
RA: 6.	**Multiple Working:** TDM system.

Class 86 were formerly numbered E 3101–3200 (not in order).

Class 86/1. Class 87-type bogies & motors.
Details as above except:
Maximum Tractive Effort: 258 kN (58000 lbf).
Traction Motors: GEC 412AZ frame mounted.
Continuous Rating: 3730 kW (5000 h.p.) giving a tractive effort of 95 kN (21300 lbf) at 87 m.p.h.
Maximum Rail Power: 5860 kW (7860 h.p.) at 50.8 m.p.h.

Weight: 86.8 t.	**Wheel Diameter:** 1150 mm.
Design Speed: 110 m.p.h.	**Maximum Speed:** 110 m.p.h.

86101	I		H	DFNC	CE	Sir William A Stanier FRS
86102	I		H	DFNC	CE	Robert A Riddles
86103	x	I	H	SAXL	ZH	André Chapelon

Class 86/2. Standard Design. Details as in main class heading except:
Weight: 85–86.2 t.

Note: Locomotives from pool WEOE may be loaned on a day-to-day basis to West Coast Traincare for operation by Virgin West Cost in pool IWPA.

86204	I		H	SAXL	ZH	City of Carlisle
86205	V		H	IWPA	WN	City of Lancaster
86206	V		H	ICCA	LG	City of Stoke on Trent
86207	I		H	ICCA	LG	City of Lichfield
86208	I		E	WNXX	CE	City of Chester
86209	V		H	ICCA	LG	City of Coventry
86210	x	**RX**	E	WEOE	CE	C.I.T. 75th Anniversary
86212	V		H	ICCA	LG	Preston Guild 1328–1992

86213	V	H	SAXL	CP	Lancashire Witch
86214	I	H	ICCA	LG	Sans Pareil
86215	AR	H	IANA	NC	
86216	I	H	SAXL	ZH	Meteor
86217	AR	H	IANA	NC	City University
86218	AR	H	IANA	NC	NHS 50
86219	I	H	SAXL	ZH	Phoenix
86220	AR	H	IANA	NC	The Round Tabler
86221	AR	H	IANA	NC	B.B.C. Look East
86222	V	H	ICCA	LG	Clothes Show Live
86223	AR	H	IANA	NC	Norwich Union
86224	I	H	ICCA	LG	
86225	V	H	ICCA	LG	Hardwicke
86226	V	H	ICCA	LG	CHARLES RENNIE MACKINTOSH
86227	I	H	SAXL	ZH	Sir Henry Johnson
86228	V	H	SAXL	CP	Vulcan Heritage
86229	V	H	IWPA	WN	Lions Clubs International
86230	AR	H	IANA	NC	
86231	V	H	ICCA	LG	Starlight Express
86232	AR	H	IANA	NC	
86233	V	H	IWPA	WN	Laurence Olivier
86234	I	H	IANA	NC	J B Priestley OM
86235	AR	H	IANA	NC	Crown Point
86236	V	H	ICCA	LG	Josiah Wedgwood
86237	AR	H	IANA	NC	University of East Anglia
86238	AR	H	IANA	NC	European Community
86240	V	H	ICCA	LG	Bishop Eric Treacy
86241	RX	E	WNXX	CE	Glenfiddich
86242	V	H	ICCA	LG	James Kennedy GC
86243 x	RX	E	WEOE	CE	
86244	V	H	ICCA	LG	
86245	V	H	IWPA	WN	
86246	AR	H	IANA	NC	
86247	V	H	IWPA	WN	Abraham Darby
86248	V	H	ICCA	LG	Sir Clwyd/County of Clwyd
86249	I	H	ICCA	LG	County of Merseyside
86250	AR	H	IANA	NC	
86251	V	H	ICCA	LG	The Birmingham Post
86252	AR	H	IANA	NC	Sheppard 100
86253	I	H	ICCA	LG	The Manchester Guardian
86254 x	RX	E	WEOE	CE	
86255	I	H	SAXL	PC	Penrith Beacon
86256	V	H	ICCA	LG	Pebble Mill
86257	AR	H	IANA	NC	
86258	V	H	ICCA	LG	Talyllyn 50 Years of Railway Preservation 2001
86259	V	H	IWPA	WN	Greater MANCHESTER THE LIFE & SOUL OF BRITAIN
86260	V	H	IWPA	WN	Driver Wallace Oakes G.C.
86261 x	E	E	WEOE	CE	THE RAIL CHARTER PARTNERSHIP

Class 86/4. EWS owned locomotives. Details as Class 86/2 except:
Traction Motors: AEI 282AZ axle hung.
Maximum Tractive Effort: 258 kN (58000 lbf).
Weight: 83–83.9 t.
Continuous Rating: 2680 kW (3600 h.p.) giving a tractive effort of 89 kN (20000 lbf) at 67 m.p.h.
Maximum Rail Power: 4400 kW (5900 h.p.) at 38 m.p.h.
Note: Locomotives from pool WEOE may be loaned on a day-to-day basis to West Coast Traincare for operation by Virgin West Cost in pool IWPA.

86401	**E**	E	WEOE	CE	Hertfordshire Rail Tours
86416 x	**RX**	E	WEOE	CE	
86417 x	**RX**	E	WNXX	CE	
86419 x	**RX**	E	WNXX	CE	
86424	**RX**	E	WEOE	CE	
86425	**RX**	E	WEOE	CE	Saint Mungo
86426 x	**E**	E	WEOE	CE	Pride of the Nation
86430 x	**RX**	E	WEOE	CE	Saint Edmund

Class 86/5. Regeared locomotive operated by Freightliner.
Details as Class 86/4 except:
Continuous Rating: 2680 kW (3600 h.p.) giving a tractive effort of 117 kN (26300 lbf) at 67 m.p.h.
Maximum Speed: 75 m.p.h.   **Train Supply:** Electric, isolated.

86501 (86608)	**FL**	FL	DFGC	CE	

Class 86/6. Freightliner operated locomotives. Details as Class 86/4 except:
Maximum Speed: 75 m.p.h.   **Train Supply:** Electric, isolated.

86602	**FL**	FL	DFNC	CE	
8660?	**FE**	FL	DHLT	CE	
86604	**FF**	FL	DFNC	CE	
86605	**FF**	FL	DFNC	CE	
86606	**FF**	FL	DHLT	CE	
86607	**FL**	FL	DFNC	CE	
86609	**FL**	FL	DFNC	CE	
86610	**F**	FL	DFNC	CE	
86611	**FF**	FL	DFNC	CE	Airey Neave
86612	**FF**	P	DFNC	CE	Elizabeth Garrett Anderson
86613	**FL**	P	DFNC	CE	
86614	**FF**	P	DFNC	CE	
86615	**F**	P	DFNC	CE	Rotary International
86618	**FF**	P	DHLT	CE	
86620	**FL**	P	DFNC	CE	Philip G Walton
86621	**FF**	P	DFNC	CE	London School of Economics
86622	**FF**	P	DFNC	CE	
86623	**FF**	P	DFNC	CE	
86627	**FL**	P	DFNC	CE	
86628	**FF**	P	DFNC	CE	Aldaniti
86631	**FL**	P	DFNC	CE	
86632	**FL**	P	DFNC	CE	
86633	**FF**	P	DFNC	CE	Wulfruna

86634	**FL**	P	DFNC	CE
86635	**FL**	P	DFNC	CE
86636	**FL**	P	DHLT	CE
86637	**FF**	P	DFNC	CE
86638	**FF**	P	DFNC	CE
86639	**FF**	P	DFNC	CE

CLASS 87   BREL/GEC   Bo-Bo

Built: 1973–75 by BREL at Crewe Works.
Electric Supply System: 25 kV a.c. 50 Hz overhead.
Traction Motors: GEC G412AZ frame mounted.
Maximum Tractive Effort: 258 kN (58000 lbf).
Continuous Rating: 3730 kW (5000 h.p.) giving a tractive effort of 95 kN (21300 lbf) at 87 m.p.h.
Maximum Rail Power: 5860 kW (7860 h.p.) at 50.8 m.p.h.
Train Brakes: Air.   **Brake Force:** 40 t.
Dimensions: 17.83 x 2.65 m.   **Weight:** 83.3 t.
Wheel Diameter: 1150 mm.   **Design Speed:** 110 m.p.h.
Maximum Speed: 110 m.p.h.   **Train Supply:** Electric, index 95.
RA: 6.   **Multiple Working:** TDM system.

87001	**V**	P	IWCA	WN	Royal Scot
87002	**V**	P	IWCA	WN	Royal Sovereign
87003	**V**	P	IWCA	WN	Patriot
87004	**V**	P	IWCA	WN	Britannia
87005	**V**	P	IWCA	WN	City of London
87006	**V**	P	IWCA	WN	George Reynolds
87007	**V**	P	IWCA	WN	City of Manchester
87008	**V**	P	IWCA	WN	City of Liverpool
87009	**V**	P	IWCA	WN	City of Birmingham
87010	**V**	P	IWCA	WN	King Arthur
87011	**V**	P	IWCA	WN	City of Wolverhampton
87012	**V**	P	IWCA	WN	Coeur de Lion
87013	**V**	P	IWCA	WN	John O'Gaunt
87014	**V**	P	IWCA	WN	Knight of the Thistle
87015	**V**	P	IWCA	WN	Howard of Effingham
87016	**V**	P	IWCA	WN	Willesden Intercity Depot
87017	**V**	P	IWCA	WN	Iron Duke
87018	**V**	P	IWCA	WN	Lord Nelson
87019	**V**	P	IWCA	WN	Sir Winston Churchill
87020	**V**	P	IWCA	WN	North Briton
87021	**V**	P	IWCA	WN	Robert The Bruce
87022	**V**	P	IWCA	WN	Lew Adams The Black Prince
87023	**V**	P	IWCA	WN	Polmadie
87024	**V**	P	IWCA	WN	Lord of the Isles
87025	**V**	P	IWCA	WN	County of Cheshire
87026	**V**	P	IWCA	WN	Sir Richard Arkwright
87027	**V**	P	IWCA	WN	Wolf of Badenoch

87028	V	P	IWCA	WN	Lord President
87029	V	P	IWCA	WN	Earl Marischal
87030	V	P	IWCA	WN	Black Douglas
87031	V	P	IWCA	WN	Hal o' the Wynd
87032	V	P	IWCA	WN	Kenilworth
87033	V	P	IWCA	WN	Thane of Fife
87034	V	P	IWCA	WN	William Shakespeare
87035	V	P	IWCA	WN	Robert Burns

CLASS 89   BRUSH   Co-Co

Built: 1986 by BREL at Crewe Works (as sub-contractors for Brush).
Electric Supply System: 25 kV a.c. 50 Hz overhead.
Traction Motors: Brush. Frame mounted.
Maximum Tractive Effort: 205 kN (46000 lbf).
Continuous Rating: 4350 kW (5850 h.p.) giving a tractive effort of 105 kN (23600 lbf) at 92 m.p.h.

Maximum Rail Power:
Brake Force: 50 t.
Weight: 104 t.
Design Speed: 125 m.p.h.
Train Supply: Electric, index 95.
Multiple Working: TDM system.

Train Brakes: Air.
Dimensions: 19.80 x 2.74 m.
Wheel Diameter: 1150 mm.
Maximum Speed: 125 m.p.h.
RA: 6.

| 89001 | **GN** | SI | IECB | BN |

CLASS 90   GEC   Bo-Bo

Built: 1987–90 by BREL at Crewe Works (as sub contractors for GEC).
Electric Supply System: 25 kV a.c. 50 Hz overhead.
Traction Motors: GEC G412CY frame mounted.
Maximum Tractive Effort: 258 kN (58000 lbf).
Continuous Rating: 3730 kW (5000 h.p.) giving a tractive effort of 95 kN (21300 lbf) at 87 m.p.h.
Maximum Rail Power: 5860 kW (7860 h.p.) at 68.3 m.p.h.
Train Brakes: Air.
Brake Force: 40 (* 50) t.
Weight: 84.5 t.
Design Speed: 110 m.p.h.
Train Supply: Electric, index 95.
Multiple Working: TDM system.
Non-standard liveries:

Dimensions: 18.80 x 2.74 m.
Wheel Diameter: 1156 mm.
Maximum Speed: 110 (* 100) m.p.h.
RA: 7.

90028 is in Belgian Railways style blue and yellow.
90029 is in German Federal Railways style raspberry red and white.
90036 is as **FE**, but has a yellow roof.

Class 90/0. Standard Design. Details as above.

90001	b	**V**	P	IWCA	WN	BBC Midlands Today
90002	b	**V**	P	IWCA	WN	Mission: Impossible
90003	b	**V**	P	IWCA	WN	THE HERALD
90004	b	**V**	P	IWCA	WN	City of Glasgow
90005	b	**V**	P	IWCA	WN	Financial Times
90006	b	**V**	P	IWCA	WN	Modern Railways Magazine/ Roger Ford
90007	b	**V**	P	IWCA	WN	Lord Stamp
90008	b	**V**	P	IWCA	WN	The Birmingham Royal Ballet
90009	b	**V**	P	IWCA	WN	The Economist
90010	b	**V**	P	IWCA	WN	275 Railway Squadron (Volunteers)
90011	b	**V**	P	IWCA	WN	West Coast Rail 250
90012	b	**V**	P	IWCA	WN	British Transport Police
90013	b	**V**	P	IWCA	WN	The Law Society
90014	b	**V**	P	IWCA	WN	
90015	b	**V**	P	IWCA	WN	The International Brigades SPAIN 1936–1939
90016	†b	**RX**	E	WEFE	CE	
90017	†b	**RX**	E	WEFE	CE	Rail express systems Quality Assured
90018	†b	**RX**	E	WEFE	CE	
90019	†b	**RX**	E	WEFE	CE	Penny Black
90020	†b	**E**	E	WEFE	CE	Sir Michael Heron
90026	†	**FE**	EF	WEFE	CE	Crewe International Electric Maintenance Depot
90028	†	**O**	EF	WEFE	CE	Vrachtverbinding
90029	†	**O**	EF	WEFE	CE	Frachtverbindungen
90030	†	**E**	EF	WEFE	CE	Crewe Locomotive Works
90031	†	**E**	EF	WEFE	CE	The Railway Children Partnership Working For Street Children Worldwide
90032	†	**FE**	EF	WEFE	CE	Cerestar
90034	†	**FE**	EF	WEFE	CE	
90035	†	**FE**	EF	WEFE	CE	
90036	†	**O**	EF	WEFE	CE	
90037	†	**F**	EF	WEFE	CE	Spirit of Dagenham
90040	†	**F**	EF	WEFE	CE	The Railway Mission

Class 90/1. Freightliner leased locomotives. Details as Class 90/0 except:
Maximum Speed: 75 m.p.h.   **Train Supply**: Electric, isolated.

90141	**FF**	P	DFLC	CE	
90142	**FF**	P	DFLC	CE	
90143	**FF**	P	DFLC	CE	Freightliner Coatbridge
90144	**FF**	P	DFLC	CE	
90145	**FF**	P	DFLC	CE	
90146	**FF**	P	IWCA	CE	
90147	**FF**	P	DFLC	CE	
90148	**FF**	P	DFLC	CE	
90149	**FF**	P	DFLC	CE	
90150	**FF**	P	DFLC	CE	

Class 90/2. EWS locomotives fitted with composition brake blocks. Details as Class 90/0 except:
Brake Force: 50 tons.

Note: One (unspecified) locomotive is hired from EWS (Pool WEPE) to Great North Eastern Railway (Pool IECA) on a regular basis. This locomotive is used between London King's Cross and Leeds/Bradford Forster Square only.

90221	(90021)	**FE**	EF	WEPE	CE
90222	(90022)	**FE**	EF	WEPE	CE
90223	(90023)	**FE**	EF	WEPE	CE
90224	(90024)	**GN**	EF	WEPE	CE
90225	(90025)	**FF**	EF	WEPE	CE
90227	(90027)	**F**	EF	WEPE	CE
90233	(90033)	**FE**	EF	WEPE	CE
90238	(90038)	**FE**	EF	WEPE	CE
90239	(90039)	**F**	EF	WEPE	CE

CLASS 91   GEC   Bo-Bo

Built: 1988–91 by BREL at Crewe Works (as sub contractors for GEC).
Electric Supply System: 25 kV a.c. 50 Hz overhead.
Traction Motors: GEC G426AZ.   **Maximum Tractive Effort:**
Continuous Rating: 4540 kW (6090 h.p.) giving a tractive effort of ?? kN at ?? m.p.h.
Maximum Rail Power: 4700 kW (6300 h.p.) at ?? m.p.h.
Train Brakes: Air.
Brake Force: 45 t.   **Dimensions:** 19.41 x 2.74 m.
Weight: 84 t.   **Wheel Diameter:** 1000 mm.
Design Speed: 140 m.p.h.   **Maximum Speed:** 125 m.p.h.
Train Supply: Electric, index 95.   **RA:** 7.
Multiple Working: TDM system.

Note: This class is in the process of refurbishment at Bombardier, Doncaster. Refurbished locomotives are reclassified 91/1 and have been renumbered by the addition of 100 to their existing number.

91101	**GN**	H	IECA	BN	
91002	**GN**	H	IECA	BN	Durham Cathedral
91103	**GN**	H	IECA	BN	County of Lincolnshire
91004	**GN**	H	IECA	BN	Grantham
91105	**GN**	H	IECA	BN	County of Durham
91106	**GN**	H	IECA	BN	East Lothian
91107	**GN**	H	IECA	BN	Newark-on-Trent
91008	**GN**	H	IECA	BN	
91109	**GN**	H	IECA	BN	Samaritans
91110	**GN**	H	IECA	BN	David Livingstone
91011	**GN**	H	IECA	BN	Terence Cuneo
91012	**GN**	H	IECA	BN	County of Cambridgeshire
91013	**GN**	H	IECA	BN	County of North Yorkshire
91014	**GN**	H	IECA	BN	St. Mungo Cathedral

▲ Class 58 No. 58042 in Mainline blue livery at Worksop depot on 21/06/1998. This loco is, at the time of writing, the only member of this class in this livery still in active service. **Michael Hill**

▼ Class 59/2 No. 59203 'Vale of Pickering' at Reading with the 10.33 Sevington–Merehead. **Kevin Conkey**

Class 60 No. 60007 in Loadhaul livery works the 12.29 Fidlers Ferry PS–Arpley m.g.r empties past Monks Sidings on the Warrington Low Level line.
Doug Birmingham

▲ GB Railfreight Class 66/7 No. 66706 at Toton Virtual Quarry with the 13.15 ex-Mountsorrel on 08/08/2001. **Paul Robertson**

▼ South West Trains' "Thunderbird", electro-diesel 73109 'Battle of Britain 50th Anniversary' in Stagecoach livery hauls a Wimbledon–Bournemouth e.c.s., consisting of a Class 423 unit, past Winchester on 21/05/2001. **Brian Denton**

67005 'Queen's Messenger' at the head of the 15.58 London Paddington–Plymouth mail on 28/08/2001. **Anthony Kay**

Freightliner's unique re-geared 86501 passes Norton Bridge with the 07.34 Crewe–Grain freightliner on 22/06/2001.

Hugh Ballantyne

▲ Virgin-liveried 87017 'Iron Duke' passes Stafford station with the 14.30 London Euston–Glasgow Central on 24/06/2001. **Hugh Ballantyne**

▼ EWS Class 90/2 No. 90227 'Allerton T&RS Depot' passes Motherwell with empty vans for Shieldmuir on 18/05/2001. **Mark Beal**

Class 91 91008 works the 15.30 GNER service from London Kings Cross to Newcastle past Burn on 20/08/2001.
Doug Birmingham

One of two EWS-liveried 92001 'Victor Hugo' passes Kemsing with the 09.33 Wembley–Dollands Moor international service on 31/08/1999.

Rodney Lissenden

91015	**GN**	H	IECA	BN	Holyrood
91116	**GN**	H	IECA	BN	
91017	**GN**	H	IECA	BN	City of Leeds
91018	**GN**	H	IECA	BN	Bradford Film Festival
91019	**GN**	H	IECA	BN	County of Tyne & Wear
91120	**GN**	H	IECA	BN	
91021	**GN**	H	IECA	BN	Archbishop Thomas Cranmer
91022	**GN**	H	IECA	BN	Double Trigger
91023	**GN**	H	IECA	BN	
91024	**GN**	H	IECA	BN	Reverend W Awdry
91025	**GN**	H	IECA	BN	Berwick-upon-Tweed
91026	**GN**	H	IECA	BN	York Minster
91127	**GN**	H	IECA	BN	Edinburgh Castle
91028	**GN**	H	IECA	BN	Peterborough Cathedral
91029	**GN**	H	IECA	BN	Queen Elizabeth II
91130	**GN**	H	IECA	BN	City of Newcastle
91031	**GN**	H	IECA	BN	County of Northumberland

CLASS 92   BRUSH   Co-Co

Built: 1993–96 by Brush Traction at Loughborough.
Electric Supply System: 25 kV a.c. 50 HZ overhead or 750 V d.c. third rail.
Traction Motors: Brush.
Maximum Tractive Effort: 400 kN (90 000 lbf).
Continuous Rating: 5040 kW (6760 h.p.) on a.c., 4000 kW (5360 h.p.) on d.c.
Maximum Rail Power: 126 t.   **Train Brakes:** Air.
Brake Force: 63 t.   **Dimensions:** 21.34 x 2.67 m.
Weight: 126 t.   **Wheel Diameter:** 1160 mm.
Design Speed: 140 km/h (87 m.p.h.).   **Maximum Speed:** 140 km/h (87 m.p.h.).
Train Supply: Electric, index 108 (a.c.), 70 (d.c.).
RA: 7.

Note: Locomotives in pool WTWE are also authorised to operate on the Eurotunnel network. These locomotives have temporarily had their d.c. shoegear removed and may only operate under power between Dollands Moor and Fréthun.

92001	**E**	E	WTWE	CE	Victor Hugo
92002	**EP**	E	WTWE	CE	H.G. Wells
92003	**EP**	E	WTWE	CE	Beethoven
92004	**EP**	E	WTAE	CE	Jane Austen
92005	**EP**	E	WTAE	CE	Mozart
92006	**EP**	SF	WTAE	CE	Louis Armand
92007	**EP**	E	WTAE	CE	Schubert
92008	**EP**	E	WTAE	CE	Jules Verne
92009	**EP**	E	WTAE	CE	Elgar
92010	**EP**	SF	WTWE	CE	Molière
92011	**EP**	E	WTAE	CE	Handel
92012	**EP**	E	WTWE	CE	Thomas Hardy
92013	**EP**	E	WTAE	CE	Puccini
92014	**EP**	SF	WTAE	CE	Emile Zola

92015	EP	E	WTAE	CE	D.H. Lawrence
92016	EP	E	WTAE	CE	Brahms
92017	EP	E	WTAE	CE	Shakespeare
92018	EP	SF	WTAE	CE	Stendhal
92019	EP	E	WTAE	CE	Wagner
92020	EP	EU	WNWX	CE	Milton
92021	EP	EU	WNWX	CE	Purcell
92022	EP	E	WTAE	CE	Charles Dickens
92023	EP	SF	WTWE	CE	Ravel
92024	EP	E	WTAE	CE	J.S. Bach
92025	EP	E	WTAE	CE	Oscar Wilde
92026	EP	E	WTAE	CE	Britten
92027	EP	E	WTAE	CE	George Eliot
92028	EP	SF	WTWE	CE	Saint Saëns
92029	EP	E	WTWE	CE	Dante
92030	EP	E	WTAE	CE	Ashford
92031	E		WTWE	CE	The Institute of Logistics and Transport
92032	EP	EU	WNWX	CE	César Franck
92033	EP	SF	WTWE	CE	Berlioz
92034	EP	E	WTAE	CE	Kipling
92035	EP	E	WTAE	CE	Mendelssohn
92036	EP	E	WTAE	CE	Bertolt Brecht
92037	EP	E	WTWE	CE	Sullivan
92038	EP	SF	WTWE	CE	Voltaire
92039	EP	E	WTWE	CE	Johann Strauss
92040	EP	EU	WNWX	CE	Goethe
92041	EP	E	WTAE	CE	Vaughan Williams
92042	EP	E	WTAE	CE	Honegger
92043	EP	SF	WTWE	CE	Debussy
92044	EP	EU	WNWX	CE	Couperin
92045	EP	EU	WNWX	CE	Chaucer
92046	EP	EU	WNWX	CE	Sweelinck

3. EUROTUNNEL LOCOMOTIVES

DIESEL LOCOMOTIVES

0001–0005   MaK   Bo-Bo

Built: 1992–93 by MaK at Kiel, Germany (Model DE1004).
Engine: MTU 12V 396 Tc of 1180 kW (1580 h.p.) at 1800 rpm.
Main Alternator: BBC.   **Traction Motors:** BBC.
Maximum Tractive Effort: 305 kN (68600 lbf).
Continuous Tractive Effort: 140 kN (31500 lbf) at 20 mph.
Power At Rail: 750 kW (1012 h.p.).
Brake Force: 120 kN.   **Dimensions:** 16.50 x ?? x ?? m.
Weight: 84 t.   **Wheel Diameter:** 1000 mm.
Design Speed: 120 km/h.   **Maximum Speed:** 120 km/h.
Fuel Capacity: **Train Brakes:** Air.
Train Supply: Not equipped.   **Multiple Working:** Within class.

0001	**GY**	ET	CO
0002	**GY**	ET	CO
0003	**GY**	ET	CO
0004	**GY**	ET	CO
0005	**GY**	ET	CO

0032–0042   HUNSLET/SCHÖMA   0-4-0

Built: 1989–90 by Hunslet Engine Company at Leeds as 900 mm. gauge.
Rebuilt: 1993-94 by Schöma in Germany to 1435 mm. gauge.
Engine: Deutz of 270 kW (200 h.p.) at ???? rpm.
Transmission: Mechanical.   **Maximum Tractive Effort:**
Cont. Tractive Effort: **Power At Rail:**
Brake Force: **Dimensions:**
Weight: **Wheel Diameter:**
Design Speed: 50 km/h.   **Maximum Speed:** 50 km/h.
Fuel Capacity: **Train Brakes:** Air.
Train Supply: Not equipped.   **Multiple Working:** Not equipped.

0031	**Y**	ET	CO	FRANCES
0032	**Y**	ET	CO	ELISABETH
0033	**Y**	ET	CO	SILKE
0034	**Y**	ET	CO	AMANDA
0035	**Y**	ET	CO	MARY
0036	**Y**	ET	CO	LAWRENCE
0037	**Y**	ET	CO	LYDIE
0038	**Y**	ET	CO	JENNY
0039	**Y**	ET	CO	PACITA
0040	**Y**	ET	CO	JILL
0041	**Y**	ET	CO	KIM
0042	**Y**	ET	CO	NICOLE

ELECTRIC LOCOMOTIVES

9001–9113   BRUSH/ABB   Bo-Bo-Bo

Built: 1993–2001 by Brush Traction at Loughborough.
Supply System: 25 kV a.c. 50 Hz overhead.
Traction Motors: ABB 6PH.   **Maximum Tractive Effort:** 400 kN (90 000 lbf).
Continuous Rating: 5760 kW (7725 h.p.) giving a TE of 310 kN at 65 km/h.
Maximum Rail Power: **Multiple Working:** TDM system.
Brake Force: 50 t.   **Dimensions:** 22.01 x 2.97 x 4.20 m.
Weight: 132 t.   **Wheel Diameter:** 1090 mm.
Design Speed: 175 km/h.   **Maximum Speed:** 160 km/h.
Train Supply: Electric.   **Train Brakes:** Air.

CLASS 9/0. Mixed traffic locomotives.

9001	**ET**	ET	CO	LESLEY GARRETT
9002	**ET**	ET	CO	STUART BURROWS
9003	**ET**	ET	CO	BENJAMIN LUXON
9004	**ET**	ET	CO	VICTORIA DE LOS ANGELES
9005	**ET**	ET	CO	JESSYE NORMAN
9006	**ET**	ET	CO	REGINE CRESPIN
9007	**ET**	ET	CO	DAME JOAN SUTHERLAND
9008	**ET**	ET	CO	ELISABETH SODERSTROM
9009	**ET**	ET	CO	FRANÇOIS POLLET
9010	**ET**	ET	CO	JEAN-PHILLIPE COURTIS
9011	**ET**	ET	CO	JOSÉ VAN DAM
9012	**ET**	ET	CO	LUCIANO PAVAROTTI
9013	**ET**	ET	CO	MARIA CALLAS
9014	**ET**	ET	CO	LUCIA POPP
9015	**ET**	ET	CO	LÖTSCHBERG 1913
9016	**ET**	ET	CO	WILLARD WHITE
9017	**EG**	ET	CO	JOSÉ CARRERAS
9018	**ET**	ET	CO	WILHELMENA FERNANDEZ
9019	**ET**	ET	CO	MARIA EWING
9020	**ET**	ET	CO	Nicolai Ghiaurov
9021	**ET**	ET	CO	TERESA BERGANZA
9022	**ET**	ET	CO	DAME JANET BAKER
9023	**ET**	ET	CO	DAME ELISABETH LEGGE-SCHWARZKOPF
9024	**ET**	ET	CO	GOTTHARD 1882
9025	**ET**	ET	CO	JUNGFRAUJOCH 1912
9026	**ET**	ET	CO	FURKATUNNEL 1982
9027	**ET**	ET	CO	BARBARA HENDRICKS
9028	**ET**	ET	CO	DAME KIRI TE KANAWA
9029	**ET**	ET	CO	THOMAS ALLEN
9031	**ET**	ET	CO	
9032	**ET**	ET	CO	RENATA TEBALDI
9033	**ET**	ET	CO	MONTSERRAT CABALLE
9034	**ET**	ET	CO	MIRELLA FRENI
9035	**ET**	ET	CO	Nicolai Gedda

9036	**ET**	ET	CO	ALAIN FONDARY
9037	**ET**	ET	CO	GABRIEL BACQUIER
9038	**ET**	ET	CO	HILDEGARD BEHRENS
9040	**EG**	ET	CO	

CLASS 9/1. Freight Shuttle dedicated locomotives.

9101	**EG**	ET	CO
9102	**EG**	ET	CO
9103	**EG**	ET	CO
9104	**EG**	ET	CO
9105	**EG**	ET	CO
9106	**EG**	ET	CO
9107	**EG**	ET	CO
9108	**EG**	ET	CO
9109	**EB**	ET	CO
9110	**EB**	ET	CO
9111	**EB**	ET	CO
9112	**EB**	ET	CO
9113	**EB**	ET	CO

9701–9707   BRUSH/ADTRANZ   Bo-Bo-Bo

Built: 2001 by Brush Traction at Loughborough.
Supply System: 25 kV a.c. 50 Hz overhead.

Traction Motors:	**Maximum Tractive Effort:**
Continuous Rating: 7000 kW.	
Maximum Rail Power:	**Multiple Working:**
Brake Force:	**Dimensions:**
Weight:	**Wheel Diameter:**
Design Speed:	**Maximum Speed:**
Train Supply:	**Train Brakes:**

9701
9702
9703
9704
9705
9706
9707

4. CODES

4.1. LIVERY CODES

Locomotives are BR blue unless otherwise indicated. The colour of the lower half of the bodyside is stated first. Minor variations to these liveries are ignored.

* denotes an obsolescent livery style no longer normally used for repaints.

Code   *Description*

B*   BR (Blue).
BL*   BR (Blue with yellow cabs, grey roof, large numbers).
BR*   BR (Blue with red solebar stripe).
CE*   BR Engineers (Yellow & grey with black cab doors and window surrounds).
DG*   BR Departmental (Plain dark grey with black cab doors and window surrounds).
DR   Direct Rail Services (Dark blue with light blue roof).
E   English Welsh & Scottish Railway (Maroon bodyside & roof with gold stripe, gold reflective stripe at solebar level).
EB   Eurotunnel (grey with broad blue stripe).
EG   Eurotunnel (Two-tone grey and white).
EN   Enron Teesside Operations (Trafalgar blue with red solebar stripe).
EP   European Passenger Services (Two-tone grey with dark blue roof).
ET   Eurotunnel (Two-tone grey and white with green and blue bands).
F*   BR Trainload Freight (Two-tone grey with black cab doors and window surrounds. Various logos).
FE*   Railfreight Distribution International (Two tone-grey with black cab doors and dark blue roof. Red & yellow logo).
FF*   Freightliner (Two-tone grey with black cab doors and window surrounds. Freightliner logo).
FG   First Great Western (Green and ivory with thin green and broad gold stripes).
FL   Freightliner (Dark green with yellow cabs).
FR   Fragonset Railways (Black with silver roof and a red bodyside band lined out in white).
FW   First Great Western (Indigo blue with white roof and gold, pink and white stripes)
FY   Foster Yeoman (Blue/silver. Cast numberplates).
G*   BR (Plain green, with white stripe on main line locomotives).
GB   GB Railfreight (Blue with orange cantrail & solebar stripes, orange cabs).
GG*   BR (Two-tone green).
GL   First Great Western (Green with gold stripe).
GN   Great North Eastern Railway (Dark blue with a red stripe).
GW*   Great Western Railway (Green, lined out in black & orange. Cast numberplates).
GX   Gatwick Express (Dark grey/white/burgundy/white).
GY   Eurotunnel (Grey and yellow).

HA	Hanson Quarry Products (Dark blue and silver).
HN	Harry Needle Railroad Company (Grey/orange, lined out in black).
I*	BR InterCity Swallow (Dark grey/white/red/white).
IM*	BR InterCity mainline (Dark grey/white/red/light grey and yellow lower cabsides, except on shunters).
K	Plain black.
LH*	BR Loadhaul (Black with orange cabsides).
MA	Maintrain (Light blue).
ML*	BR Mainline Freight (Aircraft blue with silver stripe).
MM	Midland Main Line (Teal green with cream lower body sides and three orange stripes).
MR	Mendip Rail (Green, red & silver).
MS*	Mersey Travel departmental (Yellow/black).
N*	BR Network South East (Grey/white/red/white/blue/white).
O	Non standard liveries (See class heading for details).
P	Porterbrook Leasing Company (Purple & grey).
PC*	Pullman Car Company (Umber & cream with gold lettering).
RG*	BR Parcels (Dark grey and red).
RK	Railtrack (Green and blue).
RL	RMS Locotech (Blue & red).
RO*	Railtrack (Orange with white and grey stripes).
RP	Royal Train (Claret, lined out in red and black).
RT	RT Rail (Black, lined out in red).
RX	Rail express systems (Dark grey and red with or without blue markings).
SB*	Belgian National Railways (SNCB/NMBS-style blue with yellow stripes).
SO	Serco Railtest (Red/grey).
V	Virgin Trains (red with black doors extending into bodysides, three white lower bodysides stripes).
VP	Virgin Trains (Black with a large black & white chequered flag on the bodyside).
WA	Wabtec Rail (Black).
WN	West Anglia Great Northern Railway (White with blue, grey and orange stripes).
Y	Plain yellow.
YO*	Foster Yeoman (Blue/silver/blue. Cast numberplates).

4.2. OWNER CODES

Code   Owner

50	The Fifty Fund.
90	Deltic 9000 Locomotives Ltd.
A	Angel Trains.
AM	Alstom.
AR	Anglia Railways Train Services Ltd.
BB	Bridgend County Borough Council
BT	Bombardier Transportation.
CA	Cardiff Railway Company Ltd.
CM	Cambrian Trains Ltd.
CN	The Carriage and Traction Company Ltd.
CR	Cotswold Rail Engineering Ltd.
DP	The Deltic Preservation Society Ltd.
DR	Direct Rail Services Ltd.
E	English Welsh & Scottish Railway Ltd.
EF	EWS Finance Ltd.
EN	Enron Teesside Operations Ltd.
ET	Eurotunnel plc.
EU	Eurostar (UK) Ltd.
FL	Freightliner Ltd.
FR	Fragonset Railways Ltd.
FW	Great Western Trains Company Ltd.
FX	The Felixstowe Dock & Railway Company Ltd.
FY	Foster Yeoman Ltd.
GS	The Great Scottish & Western Railway Company Ltd.
H	HSBC Rail (UKI) Ltd.
HA	The Hanson Group Ltd.
HJ	Howard Johnston Engineering.
HL	Heritage Traction Leasing Ltd.
HN	Harry Needle Railroad Company Ltd.
HS	Harry Schneider.
HX	Halifax Asset Finance Ltd.
IR	Ian Riley Engineering.
JK	Dr. John Kennedy.
MA	Maintrain Ltd.
MD	Ministry of Defence.
ME	Merseyrail Electrics Ltd.
P	Porterbrook Leasing Company Ltd.
PD	Project Defiance Limited.
PO	Privately owned (owner undisclosed).
RC	Railcare Ltd.
RK	Railtrack
RL	RMS Locotech Ltd.
RM	Royal Mail.
RT	RT Rail Tours Ltd.
RV	Riviera Trains Ltd.
SC	South Central.

SE	Connex South Eastern
SF	SNCF (Société Nationale des Chemins de fer Français).
SI	Sea Containers Railway Services Ltd.
SO	Serco Railtest Ltd.
SW	South West Trains Ltd.
VW	West Coast Trains Ltd.
WA	Wabtec Rail Ltd.
WC	West Coast Railway Company Ltd.
WF	Western Falcon Rail.
WN	West Anglia Great Northern Railway Ltd.
X	Sold for scrap, awaiting collection or disposal.

4.3. LOCOMOTIVE OPERATING POOL CODES

Code   Pool

CDJD	Serco Railtest. Class 08.
CREL	Cotswold rail
CROL	Cotswold rail
CTLO	Cambrian Trains. Operational Fleet.
DFFT	Freightliner. Class 47 with 'Dock Mode'.
DFGC	Freightliner. Class 86/5.
DFGM	Freightliner. Class 66/5, general traffic.
DFHH	Freightliner. Class 66/5, Heavy Haul Division.
DFHZ	Freightliner. Class 57 (standard fuel capacity).
DFLC	Freightliner. Class 90/1.
DFLM	Freightliner. Class 47 (with multiple working equipment).
DFLS	Freightliner. Class 08.
DFLT	Freightliner. Class 47.
DFNC	Freightliner. Class 86/6.
DFRT	Freightliner. Class 66/5, Railtrack contract.
DFTZ	Freightliner. Class 57 (additional fuel capacity).
DHLT	Freightliner. Locomotives awaiting maintenance/repair/disposal.
GBZZ	GB Rail. General.
GPSN	Eurostar (UK). Class 73.
GPSS	Eurostar (UK). Class 08.
GPSV	Eurostar (UK). Class 37.
HBSH	Wabtec Hire Locos.
HEBD	Merseyrail Electrics. Class 73.
HFSL	Virgin Cross Country. Class 08.
HFSN	Virgin West Coast. Class 08.
HGSS	Maintrain. Class 08 (Tyseley)
HISE	Maintrain. Class 08 (Derby).
HISL	Maintrain. Class 08 (Neville Hill).

HJSE	First Great Western. Class 08 (Landore).
HJSL	First Great Western. Class 08 (Laira).
HJXX	First Great Western. Class 08 (Old Oak HST & St. Phillips Marsh).
HLSV	Cardiff Railway Company. Class 08. Hire locomotive.
HNRL	Harry Needle Railtrack Leasing. Hire locomotives.
HQXX	West Anglia Great Northern Railway. Class 03.
HWSU	South Central. Class 09.
HYSB	South West Trains. Standby locomotives.
IANA	Anglia Railways. Class 86.
ICCA	Virgin Cross Country. Class 86.
ICCP	Virgin Cross Country. Class 43.
IECA	Great North Eastern Railway. Class 91.
IECB	Great North Eastern Railway. Class 89.
IECP	Great North Eastern Railway. Class 43.
ILRA	Virgin Cross Country. Class 47.
IMLP	Midland Mainline. Class 43.
IVGA	Gatwick Express. Class 73/2.
IWCA	Virgin West Coast. Classes 87 & 90.
IWCP	Virgin West Coast. Class 43.
IWLA	First Great Western. Class 47.
IWPA	Virgin West Coast. Class 86.
IWRP	First Great Western. Class 43.
KCSI	Bombardier. Class 08 (Ilford).
KDSD	Bombardier. Class 08 (Doncaster).
KESE	Alstom. Class 08 (Eastleigh).
KGSS	Bombardier. Class 08 (Glasgow).
KWSW	Bombardier. Class 08 (Wolverton).
MBDL	Non TOC owned diesel locomotives.
MOLO	RT Rail Tours (Michael Owen).
QAED	Railtrack (Class 73).
RFSH	Wabtec. Hire fleet.
RTLO	Riviera Trains. Operational Fleet.
SAXL	HSBC Rail (UK). Off lease.
SBXL	Porterbrook Leasing. Off lease.
SCXL	Angel Trains. Off lease.
SDFR	Fragonset Railways. Operational locomotives.
SDMS	Fragonset Railways. Museum locomotives.
SDXL	Fragonset Railways. Stored locomotives.
WAAK	EWS. Class 67.
WBAH	EWS. Class 66 Anglia & Southern.
WBAI	EWS. Class 66 North Eastern (South).
WBAK	EWS. Class 66 Great Western.
WBAM	EWS. Class 66 Scotland, non-RETB equipped.
WBAN	EWS. Class 66 Midland.
WBAT	EWS. Class 66 North Eastern (North).
WBBM	EWS. Class 66 RETB equipped.
WCAI	EWS. Class 60 North Eastern (South).
WCAK	EWS. Class 60 Great Western.
WCAN	EWS. Class 60 Midland.
WCAT	EWS. Class 60 North Eastern (North).

WDAG	EWS. Class 59/2.
WEFE	EWS. Class 90 Freight.
WEOE	EWS. Class 86.
WEPE	EWS. Class 90 Royal Mail & Passenger.
WFAH	EWS. Class 58.
WGAI	EWS. Class 56 North Eastern (South).
WGAT	EWS. Class 56 North Eastern (North).
WHCD	EWS. Class 47/7 Dual braked.
WHDD	EWS. Class 47 Dual braked.
WHRD	EWS. Class 47 Special Trains.
WHTN	EWS. Class 47 Hired to Serco Railtest.
WHZX	EWS. Locomotives awaiting disposal.
WKAC	EWS. Class 37 Anglia & Southern.
WKAD	EWS. Class 37 Midlands & North West.
WKAM	EWS. Class 37 Motherwell. Non-RETB.
WKBM	EWS. Class 37 RETB equipped.
WKCD	EWS. Class 37/4 Hired to First North Western & Cardiff Railway.
WKCK	EWS. Class 37. Hired to Cardiff Railway.
WKGR	EWS. Class 37. On hire to Italy.
WKGS	EWS. Class 37. On hire to Spain.
WKSN	EWS. Class 37 Railtrack Sandite contract.
WMOC	EWS. Heritage pool.
WNWX	EWS. Main line locomotives – for major repairs.
WNXX	EWS. Main line locomotives – stored.
WNYX	EWS. Main line locomotives – authorised for component recovery.
WNZX	EWS. Main line locomotives – awaiting disposal.
WPAG	EWS. Class 73.
WSAS	EWS. Shunting locomotives (Anglia & Southern Zone).
WSAW	EWS. Shunting locomotives (on hire to Allied Steel & Wire).
WSGW	EWS. Shunting locomotives (Great Western Zone).
WSMD	EWS. Shunting locomotives (Midlands Zone).
WSNE	EWS. Shunting locomotives (North East England).
WSNW	EWS. Shunting locomotives (North West England).
WSSC	EWS. Shunting locomotives (Scotland).
WSWX	EWS. Shunting locomotives – Strategic Reserve.
WSXX	EWS. Shunting locomotives – Stored.
WSYX	EWS. Shunting locomotives – component recovery only.
WTAE	EWS. Class 92 Dollands Moor–Wembley–Mossend–Doncaster & Crewe–Trafford Park Routes.
WTWE	EWS. Class 92 Eurotunnel only.
XHSD	Direct Rail Services. Operational locomotives.
XHSS	Direct Rail Services. Stored locomotives.
XYPA	Mendip Rail. Class 59/0.
XYPO	Mendip Rail. Class 59/1.

4.4. ALLOCATION & LOCATION CODES

* denotes unofficial code.

Code	Location	Depot Operator
AN	Allerton (Liverpool) T&RSMD	EWS
AY	Ayr SD	EWS
BA	Basford Hall Yard (Crewe)	*Storage location only*
BC*	Bescot Yard	*Storage location only.*
BD	Birkenhead North T&RSMD	Merseyrail Electrics
BG*	Billingham T&RSMD	Enron Teesside Operations
BH	Barrow Hill T&RSMD	Harry Needle Railroad Company
BI	Brighton T&RSMD	South Central
BK	Barton Hill (Bristol) T&RSMD	EWS
BM	Bournemouth T&RSMD	South West Trains
BN	Bounds Green (London) T&RSMD	Great North Eastern Railway
BQ	Bury T&RSMD	East Lancashire Railway
BS	Bescot (Walsall) TMD	EWS
BW*	Barry WRD (closed)	*Storage location only*
CD	Crewe Diesel TMD	EWS
CE	Crewe International Electric T&RSMD	EWS
CF	Cardiff Canton (Loco) TMD	EWS
CG*	Crewe Gresty Lane Sidings	*Storage location only*
CL	Carlisle Upperby (closed)	*Storage location only*
CO	Coquelles (France) T&RSMD	Eurotunnel
CP	Crewe Carriage T&RSMD	London & North Western Railway
CQ	Crewe (The Railway Age) T&RSMD	Carriage & Traction Company
CS	Carnforth T&RSMD	West Coast Railway Company
CT*	Chester WRD (closed)	*Storage location only*
CU*	Carlisle Currock WRD	*Storage location only*
CW*	Crewe South Yard	*Storage location only*
CZ	Central Rivers (Burton)	Bombardier Transportation
DD*	Doncaster Wood Yard	*Storage location only*
DE*	Dewsbury T&RSMD	RMS Locotech
DF	Derby RTC	Fragonset Railways
DR	Doncaster TMD	EWS
DY	Derby Etches Park T&RSMD	Maintrain
EC	Edinburgh Craigentinny T&RSMD	Great North Eastern Railway
EH	Eastleigh T&RSMD	EWS
ES	On hire to Spain	
FB	Ferrybridge T&RSMD	EWS
FF	Forest (Brussels) T&RSMD	SNCB/NMBS
FX*	Felixstowe TMD	Felixstowe Dock & Railway Company
HE	Hornsey T&RSMD	West Anglia Great Northern
HG	Hither Green TMD	EWS
HM	Healey Mills (Wakefield) SD	EWS
IM	Immingham T&RSMD	EWS
IP	Ipswich SD	EWS
IS	Inverness T&RSMD	ScotRail
IW*	Ipswich WRD	*Storage location only*

KM	Carlisle Kingmoor T&RSMD	Direct Rail Services
KR	Kidderminster T&RSMD	Severn Valley Railway
KY	Knottingley T&RSMD	EWS
LA	Laira (Plymouth) T&RSMD	First Great Western
LB	Loughborough	Brush Traction
LE	Landore (Swansea) T&RSMD	First Great Western
LG	Longsight Electric (Manchester) T&RSMD	Cross Fleet
LO	Longsight Diesel (Manchester) TMD	First North Western
LR	Leicester SD	EWS
LT*	MoD Longtown	Ministry of Defence
MD	Merehead T&RSMD	Mendip Rail
MG	Margam (Port Talbot) SD	EWS
MH	Millerhill (Edinburgh) SD	EWS
ML	Motherwell T&RSMD	EWS
NC	Norwich Crown Point T&RSMD	Anglia Railways
NL	Neville Hill InterCity (Leeds) T&RSMD	Maintrain
OC	Old Oak Common (London) TMD	EWS
OM	Old Oak Common (London) CARMD	First Great Western
OO	Old Oak Common HST T&RSMD (London)	First Great Western
OY	Oxley T&RSMD (Wolverhampton)	West Coast Traincare
PC	Polmadie T&RSMD (Glasgow)	West Coast Traincare
PM	St. Phillips Marsh (Bristol) T&RSMD	First Great Western
PY*	MoD, DERA, Pig's Bay (Shoeburyness)	*Storage location only*
RL	Ropley T&RSMD	Mid Hants Railway
RM	Ramsgate T&RSMD	Connex South Eastern
SL	Stewarts Lane (London) T&RSMD	Gatwick Express
SN*	Shoeburyness EMU Sidings	*Storage location only*
SP	Springs Branch (Wigan) CRDC	EWS
SU	Selhurst (Croydon) T&RSMD	South Central
SY	Saltley (Birmingham)SD	EWS
SZ	Southampton Maritime T&RSMD	Freightliner
TE	Thornaby T&RSMD	EWS
TM	Tyseley Museum T&RSMD	Fragonset Railways
TO	Toton (Nottinghamshire) TMD	EWS
TS	Tyseley (Birmingham) T&RSMD	Maintrain
TT*	Toton Training School (Notts)	*Storage location only*
TY	Tyne Yard SD	EWS
WA	Warrington Arpley SD	EWS
WN	Willesden (London) TMD	West Coast Train Care
ZA	Railway Technical Centre, Derby	Serco Railtest/AEA Technology
ZB	Doncaster Works	Wabtec
ZC	Crewe Works	Bombardier Transportation
ZD	Derby Litchurch Lane Works	Bombardier Transportation
ZF	Doncaster Works	Bombardier Transportation
ZG	Eastleigh Works	Alstom Transportation
ZH	Springburn Works, Glasgow	Alstom Transportation
ZI	Ilford	Bombardier Transportation
ZN	Wolverton Works	Alstom Transportation
ZP	Horbury (Wakefield)	Bombardier Transportation

4.5. DEPOT TYPE CODES

CARMD	Carriage Maintenance Depot.
CRDC	Component Recovery & Disposal Centre.
CSD	Carriage Servicing Depot.
SD	Servicing Depot.
TMD	Traction Maintenance Depot.
T&RSMD	Traction & Rolling Stock Depot.
WRD	Wagon Repair Depot.